The

Lineal Ascent

of

Joseph Franklin

GOODSELL:

A

Travis Wayne GOODSELL
Genealogical
Ancestry

Compiled by: Travis Wayne Goodsell

Introduction

This book is volume 1 of A Travis Wayne Goodsell Genealogical Ancestry. It contains the genealogical ancestry of Joseph Franklin Goodsell, the Great-Grandfather of Travis Wayne Goodsell. The information collected is from unknown family members, so the further back the line goes the more uncertain is the accuracy of the information. But it is clear that a lot of time and hard work in research was made to discover the family tree.

The collection is composed of three parts. The first part is the pedigree of Joseph Franklin Goodsell. The second part is the ancestral listing in book form. And the third part is an ancestry chart. No attempt was made to provide the family group sheets. This book is entirely dedicated to the lineal ancestors of Joseph Franklin Goodsell. This work was made possible with the assistance of Ancestral Quest Basics. The pages are scanned from the originals.

This work is published in a book form primarily for the benefit of Travis Wayne Goodsell. Having a printed copy of the genealogical information is more easily accessible and researchable. Travis spends much of his time searching for lines to extend and Temple ordinances to perform. In The Church of Jesus Christ of Latter-Day Saints, Temple rituals are performed by proxy for deceased ancestors. It is necessary for a welding link from the living member of The Church to family members as far back as possible. It all stems from a belief concerning one's afterlife status.

The volumes in the series are:

1. Joseph Franklin GOODSELL
2. Olive Emeline HOOPES
3. Edgar Osden FULLMER
4. Rhoda Maie CAMERON
5. Hamlin Hannibal SMITH
6. Rhoda Elizabeth PERRY
7. Nathan Melvin YEARSLEY
8. Josephine JONES

Pedigree Chart

8 John GOODSELL-65   2
R: 19 Jul 1767
P: Salehurst,Sussex,England
M: 16 Oct 1791 - 33
P: Hastings,Sussex,England
D: 4 Oct 1840
P: Hastings,Sussex,England

4 John GOODSELL-32
B: 24 Jul 1793
P: Hastings,Sussex,England
M: 28 Dec 1833 - 16
P: Hastings,Sussex,E,United Kingdom
D: 12 Sep 1855
P: St.Mary Magdalen,SL,Sussex,England

9 Frances BOOTS-66   3
R: 29 Dec 1771
P: Salehurst,Sussex,England
D: 2 Nov 1852
P: St. Mary In The Castle,Hastings,S,England

2 Alfred GOODSELL-16
B: 5 Jan 1851
P: Hastings,Sussex,England
M: 25 Jul 1870 - 8
P: Newton,Cache,UT,United States
D: 29 Jul 1898
P: Newton,Cache,Utah,United States

10 John BALLARD-67   4
B: 20 Feb 1784
P: Burwash,Sussex,England
M: 1 May 1809 - 34
P: Dallington,Sussex,England
D: 1855
P: Ashburnham,Sussex,England

5 Lydia Mary BALLARD-33
B: 24 Oct 1814
P: Ashburnham,Sussex,England
D: 12 Feb 1885
P: Newton,Cache,UT,United States

11 Mary HOBDEN-68   5
B: 2 Feb 1790
P: Battle,Sussex,England
D: 15 Mar 1833
P: Ashburnham,Sussex,England

1 Joseph Franklin GOODSELL-8
B: 21 Feb 1886
P: Newton,Cache,UT,United States
M: 4 Oct 1905 - 4
P: Logan City,Cache,Utah
D: 21 Sep 1934
P: Port Angeles,Clallam,W,United States

Olive Emeline HOOPES-9
(Spouse of no. 1)

12 Jens MADSEN-69   6
B: Abt 1799
P: Vejby,Frederiksborg,Denmark
M: Abt 1824 - 35
P: ,,Den
D: 27 Apr 1841
P: Vejby,Frederiksborg,Denmark

6 Hans JENSEN-34
B: 6 Aug 1825
P: Vejby,Holbo,Frederiksborg,Denmark
M: 2 May 1853 - 17
P: Hillerød,Frederiksborg,Denmark
D:
P: Vejby,V,H,Frederiksborg, Denmark

13 Pernille HANSDATTER-70   7
B: 4 Mar 1789
P: Tågerup,Ramløse,Frederiksborg,Denmark
D: 13 Jun 1867
P: Vejby,Frederiksborg,Denmark

3 Hannah Christina JENSEN-17
B: 24 Aug 1853
P: Mønge,Vejby,Frederiksborg,Denmark
D: 17 Jun 1888
P: Newton,Cache,UT,United States

14 Lars NIELSEN-71   8
B: 14 Jan 1793
P: Husby,Husby,Odense,Denmark
M: 26 Feb 1825 - 36
P: Husby,Husby,Odense,Denmark
D: 17 May 1872
P: Kindstrup,Gelsted,V,Odense, Denmark

7 Maren LARSDATTER-35
B: 29 Jul 1830
P: Mønge,V,H,Frederiksborg, Denmark
D: 9 Feb 1906
P: Newton,Cache,Utah,United States

15 Anne Catrine HANSEN-72   9
B: 27 Jun 1801
P: Kindstrup,Gelsted,Odense,Denmark
D: 14 Jan 1841
P: Gelsted,Odense,Denmark

Pedigree Chart

No. 1 on this chart is the same as No. **8** on chart no. **1**.

8 James GUTSALL-555   **10**
R: 16 Feb 1672
P: Ewhurst,Sussex,England
M: 19 Oct 1697 - 296
P: Ewhurst,Sussex,England
D: Deceased
P:

4 John GOODSALL-284
B: 8 Mar 1710
P: Ewhurst,Sussex,England
M: 15 Jul 1733 - 147
P: St James the Great Church,E,S,England
D: Deceased
P:

9 Ann BACKWELL-556   **11**
R: 7 May 1676
P: Ewhurst,Sussex,England
D: Deceased
P:

2 Thomas GOODSALL-132
B: 1734
P: Ewhurst,Sussex,England
M: 22 Apr 1764 - 67
P: Ewhurst,Sussex,England
D: 1813
P:

10 JOBLING-557
B:
P:
M: -- 297
P:
D: Deceased
P:

5 Ann JOBLIN-285
B: 1712
P: Northumberland,England
D: 1758
P: Ewhurst,Sussex,England

11 Mrs. Joblin -558
B: Abt 1685
P: England,United Kingdom
D: Deceased
P:

1 John GOODSELL-65
R: 19 Jul 1767
P: Salehurst,Sussex,England
M: 16 Oct 1791 - 33
P: Hastings,Sussex,England
D: 4 Oct 1840
P: Hastings,Sussex,England

12 Robert GLOVER-563
B: Abt 1689
P: Salehurst,Sussex,England
M: Abt 1714 - 301
P: Salehurst,Sussex,England
D: Deceased
P:

6 John GLOVER-288
B: Abt 1723
P: Bodiam,Sussex,E,United Kingdom
M: Abt 1740 - 149
P: Bodiam,Sussex,England
D: 23 Nov 1748
P:

Frances BOOTS-66
(Spouse of no. 1)

13 Elizabeth -564
B: Abt 1693
P: Salehurst,Sussex,England
D: Deceased
P:

14
B:
P:
M:
P:
D:
P:

3 Sarah Blundell GLOVER-133
B: Abt 1743
P: Salehurst,Sussex,E,United Kingdom
D: 1812
P:

7 Mary BLUNDELL-289
B: Abt 1722
P: Bodiam,Sussex,E,United Kingdom
D: Deceased
P:

15
B:
P:
D:
P:

Pedigree Chart

No. 1 on this chart is the same as No. 9 on chart no. 1.

8 James BOOTES-565   18
B: 13 Jun 1645
P: Burwash,Sussex,England,United Kingdom
M: Abt 1698 - 302
P: Burwash,Sussex,England
D: 13 May 1705
P: Burwash,Sussex,England

4 James BOOTES-290
B: 21 May 1699
P: Burwash,Sussex,England
M: 26 Dec 1721 - 150
P: Bodiam,Sussex,England
D: 13 Aug 1741
P: Bodiam,Sussex,England

9 Susanna -566
B: Abt 1647
P: Sussex,England
D: Deceased
P:

2 Bartholomew BOOTS-134
B: 25 Apr 1736
P: Bodiam,Sussex,England
M: 17 May 1767 - 68
P: Salehurst,Sussex,England
D: 16 Sep 1806
P: Northiam,Sussex,England

10 William COLLINS-567   20
B: 5 Jun 1672
P: Bodiam,Sussex,England
M: 1 Jul 1690 - 303
P: Bodiam,Sussex,England
D: Deceased
P:

5 Anne COLLINS-291
B: 4 Nov 1693
P: Bodiam,Sussex,England
D: Aft 1736
P: Bodiam,Sussex,England

11 Susanna SMERSWELL-568   21
B: 1661
P: Bodiam,Sussex,England,United Kingdom
D: Deceased
P:

1 Frances BOOTS-66
R: 29 Dec 1771
P: Salehurst,Sussex,England
M: 16 Oct 1791 - 33
P: Hastings,Sussex,England
D: 2 Nov 1852
P: St. Mary In The Castle,H,S,England

12
B:
P:
M:
P:
D:
P:

6
B:
P:
M:
P:
D:
P:

John GOODSELL-65
(Spouse of no. 1)

13
B:
P:
D:
P:

14
B:
P:
M:
P:
D:
P:

3 Elizabeth ALLEN-135
B: 1740
P: Salehurst,Sussex,E,United Kingdom
D: 5 Sep 1782
P: Salehurst,Sussex,England

7
B:
P:
D:
P:

15
B:
P:
D:
P:

Pedigree Chart

No. 1 on this chart is the same as No. **10** on chart no. **1**.

Chart no. **4**

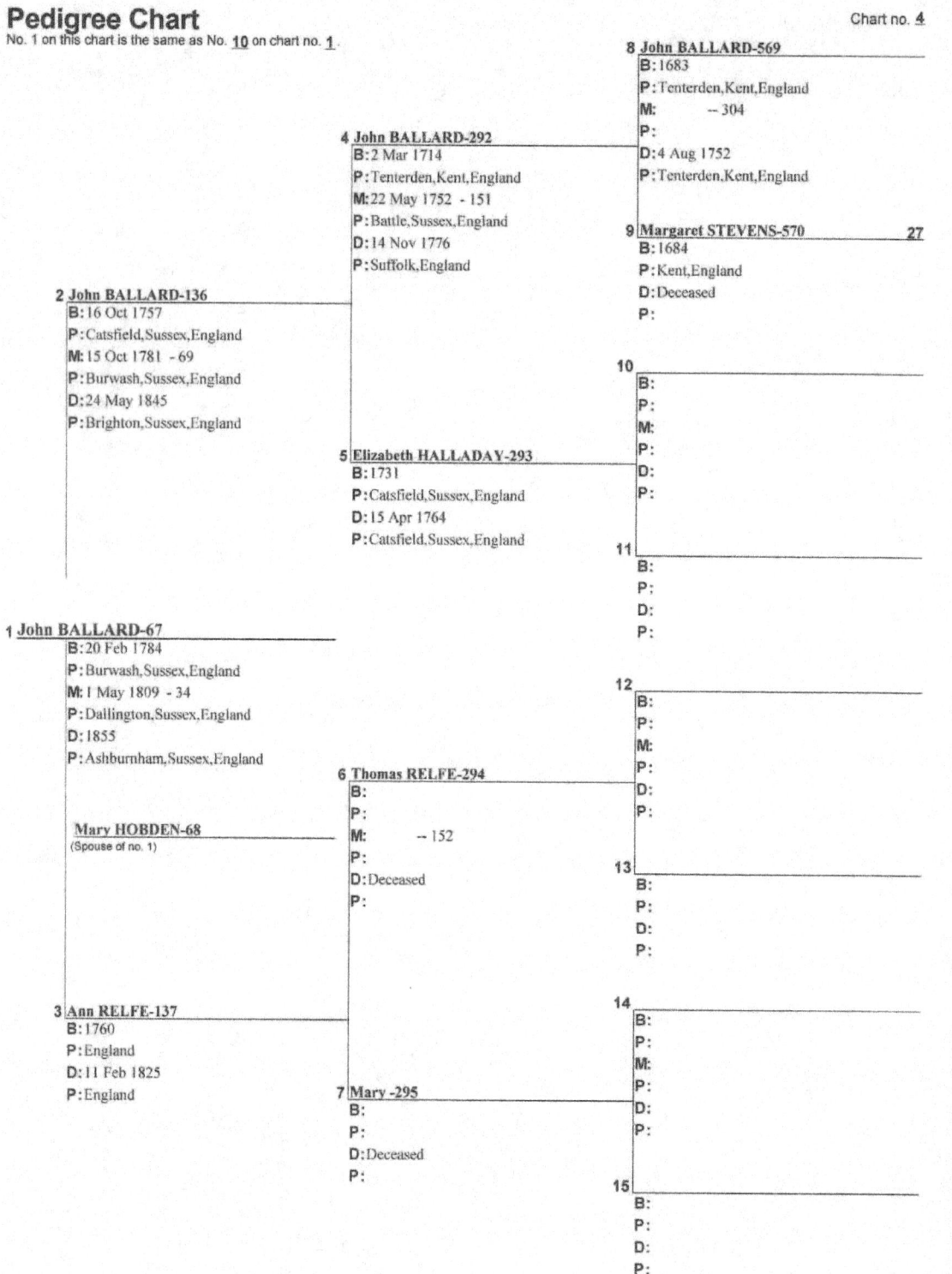

8 John BALLARD-569
B: 1683
P: Tenterden,Kent,England
M: -- 304
P:
D: 4 Aug 1752
P: Tenterden,Kent,England

4 John BALLARD-292
B: 2 Mar 1714
P: Tenterden,Kent,England
M: 22 May 1752 - 151
P: Battle,Sussex,England
D: 14 Nov 1776
P: Suffolk,England

9 Margaret STEVENS-570   27
B: 1684
P: Kent,England
D: Deceased
P:

2 John BALLARD-136
B: 16 Oct 1757
P: Catsfield,Sussex,England
M: 15 Oct 1781 - 69
P: Burwash,Sussex,England
D: 24 May 1845
P: Brighton,Sussex,England

10
B:
P:
M:
P:
D:
P:

5 Elizabeth HALLADAY-293
B: 1731
P: Catsfield,Sussex,England
D: 15 Apr 1764
P: Catsfield,Sussex,England

11
B:
P:
D:
P:

1 John BALLARD-67
B: 20 Feb 1784
P: Burwash,Sussex,England
M: I May 1809 - 34
P: Dallington,Sussex,England
D: 1855
P: Ashburnham,Sussex,England

12
B:
P:
M:
P:
D:
P:

6 Thomas RELFE-294
B:
P:
M: -- 152
P:
D: Deceased
P:

Mary HOBDEN-68
(Spouse of no. 1)

13
B:
P:
D:
P:

3 Ann RELFE-137
B: 1760
P: England
D: 11 Feb 1825
P: England

14
B:
P:
M:
P:
D:
P:

7 Mary -295
B:
P:
D: Deceased
P:

15
B:
P:
D:
P:

Pedigree Chart

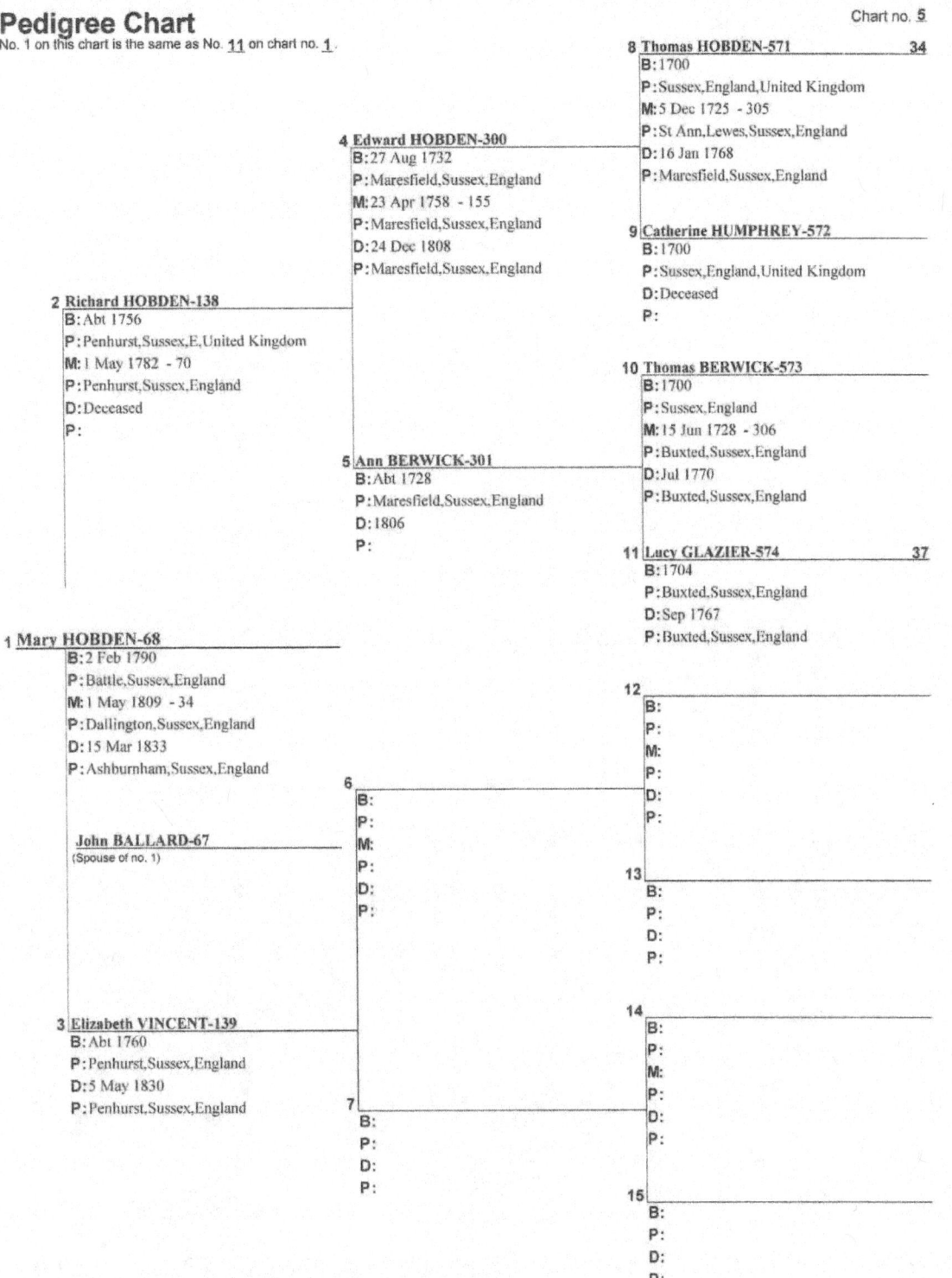

8 Thomas HOBDEN-571   **34**
B: 1700
P: Sussex,England,United Kingdom
M: 5 Dec 1725 - 305
P: St Ann,Lewes,Sussex,England
D: 16 Jan 1768
P: Maresfield,Sussex,England

4 Edward HOBDEN-300
B: 27 Aug 1732
P: Maresfield,Sussex,England
M: 23 Apr 1758 - 155
P: Maresfield,Sussex,England
D: 24 Dec 1808
P: Maresfield,Sussex,England

9 Catherine HUMPHREY-572
B: 1700
P: Sussex,England,United Kingdom
D: Deceased
P:

2 Richard HOBDEN-138
B: Abt 1756
P: Penhurst,Sussex,E,United Kingdom
M: 1 May 1782 - 70
P: Penhurst,Sussex,England
D: Deceased
P:

10 Thomas BERWICK-573
B: 1700
P: Sussex,England
M: 15 Jun 1728 - 306
P: Buxted,Sussex,England
D: Jul 1770
P: Buxted,Sussex,England

5 Ann BERWICK-301
B: Abt 1728
P: Maresfield,Sussex,England
D: 1806
P:

11 Lucy GLAZIER-574   **37**
B: 1704
P: Buxted,Sussex,England
D: Sep 1767
P: Buxted,Sussex,England

1 Mary HOBDEN-68
B: 2 Feb 1790
P: Battle,Sussex,England
M: 1 May 1809 - 34
P: Dallington,Sussex,England
D: 15 Mar 1833
P: Ashburnham,Sussex,England

12
B:
P:
M:
P:
D:
P:

6
B:
P:
M:
P:
D:
P:

13
B:
P:
D:
P:

John BALLARD-67
(Spouse of no. 1)

14
B:
P:
M:
P:
D:
P:

3 Elizabeth VINCENT-139
B: Abt 1760
P: Penhurst,Sussex,England
D: 5 May 1830
P: Penhurst,Sussex,England

7
B:
P:
D:
P:

15
B:
P:
D:
P:

Pedigree Chart

No. 1 on this chart is the same as No. 12 on chart no. 1.

8 Jens -575
B: 1710
P: Vejby, Frederiksborg, Denmark
M: -- 307
P:
D: Deceased
P:

4 Christopher JENSEN-302
B: 1735
P: Tibirke, Tibirke, Frederiksborg, Denmark
M: -- 156
P:
D: Deceased
P:

9
B:
P:
D:
P:

2 Mads CHRISTOPHERSEN-140
B: Abt 1761
P: Vejby, Frederiksborg, Denmark
M: Abt 1792 - 71
P: Vejby, Frederiksborg, Denmark
D: 14 Jun 1845
P: Vejby, Frederiksborg, Denmark

10 Hans -576
B: 1710
P: Tibirke, Tibirke, Frederiksborg, Denmark
M: -- 308
P:
D: Deceased
P:

5 Kirsten HANSDATTER-303
B: 1735
P: Tibirke, Tibirke, Frederiksborg, Denmark
D: Deceased
P:

11
B:
P:
D:
P:

1 Jens MADSEN-69
B: Abt 1799
P: Vejby, Frederiksborg, Denmark
M: Abt 1824 - 35
P: ., Den
D: 27 Apr 1841
P: Vejby, Frederiksborg, Denmark

12 Lars -577
B: 1695
P: Vejby, Vejby, Frederiksborg, Denmark
M: -- 309
P:
D: Deceased
P:

6 Niels LARSEN-305
B: 1717
P: Denmark
M: -- 158
P:
D: Deceased
P:

Pernille HANSDATTER-70
(Spouse of no. 1)

13
B:
P:
D:
P:

3 Bertha NIELSDATTER-141
B: Abt 1771
P: Vejby, Frederiksborg, Denmark
D: 1814
P:

14 Christians -578
B: 1705
P: Vejby, Vejby, Frederiksborg, Denmark
M: -- 310
P:
D: Deceased
P:

7 Birthe CHRISTIANSDATTER-306
B: Abt 1731
P: Vejby, Frederiksborg, Denmark
D:
P: Denmark

15 Nelie -579
B: 1705
P: Vejby, Frederiksborg, Denmark
D: Deceased
P:

06 Nov 2015

Pedigree Chart

8 Niels -580
B:1680
P:Tågerup,Ramløse,Frederiksborg,Denmark
M: -- 311
P:
D:Deceased
P:

4 Christen NIELSEN-308
B:Abt 1705
P:Tågerup,Ramløse,F,Denmark
M:Abt 1733 - 160
P:Tangerup,Ramlose,F,Denmark
D:Deceased
P:

9 Karen -581
B:1680
P:Tågerup,Ramlose,Frederiksborg,Denmark
D:Deceased
P:

2 Hans CHRISTENSEN-142
B:Abt 1754
P:Tågerup,Ramløse,F,Denmark
M:Abt 1776 - 72
P:Taagerup,Ramlose,F,Denmark
D:20 Aug 1814
P:Tågerup,Ramløse,F,Denmark

10 Hans -582
B:1685
P:Tågerup,Ramløse,Frederiksborg,Denmark
M: -- 312
P:
D:Deceased
P:

5 Kirsten HANSEN-309
B:Abt 1709
P:Tågerup,Ramløse,F,Denmark
D:Deceased
P:

11 Maren -583
B:1685
P:Tågerup,Ramløse,Frederiksborg,Denmark
D:Deceased
P:

1 Pernille HANSDATTER-70
B:4 Mar 1789
P:Tågerup,Ramløse,F,Denmark
M:Abt 1824 - 35
P:,,Den
D:13 Jun 1867
P:Vejby,Frederiksborg,Denmark

12 Jorgens -584
B:1710
P:Ramløse,Frederiksborg,Denmark
M: -- 313
P:
D:Deceased
P:

6 Lars JORGENSEN-310
B:Abt 1733
P:Ramløse,Frederiksborg,Denmark
M:<1761> - 161
P:Aagerup,Ramlose,F,Denmark
D:Deceased
P:

Jens MADSEN-69
(Spouse of no. 1)

13 Johanne -585
B:1710
P:Ramløse,Frederiksborg,Denmark
D:Deceased
P:

14 Mads -586
B:1710
P:Ramløse,Frederiksborg,Denmark
M: -- 314
P:
D:Deceased
P:

3 Susanne LARSDATTER-143
B:Abt 1748
P:Ramløse,Frederiksborg,Denmark
D:20 Feb 1819
P:

7 Pernille MADSDATTER-311
B:Abt 1737
P:Ramløse,Frederiksborg,Denmark
D:Deceased
P:

15 Susanne -587
B:1710
P:Ramløse,Frederiksborg,Denmark
D:Deceased
P:

Pedigree Chart

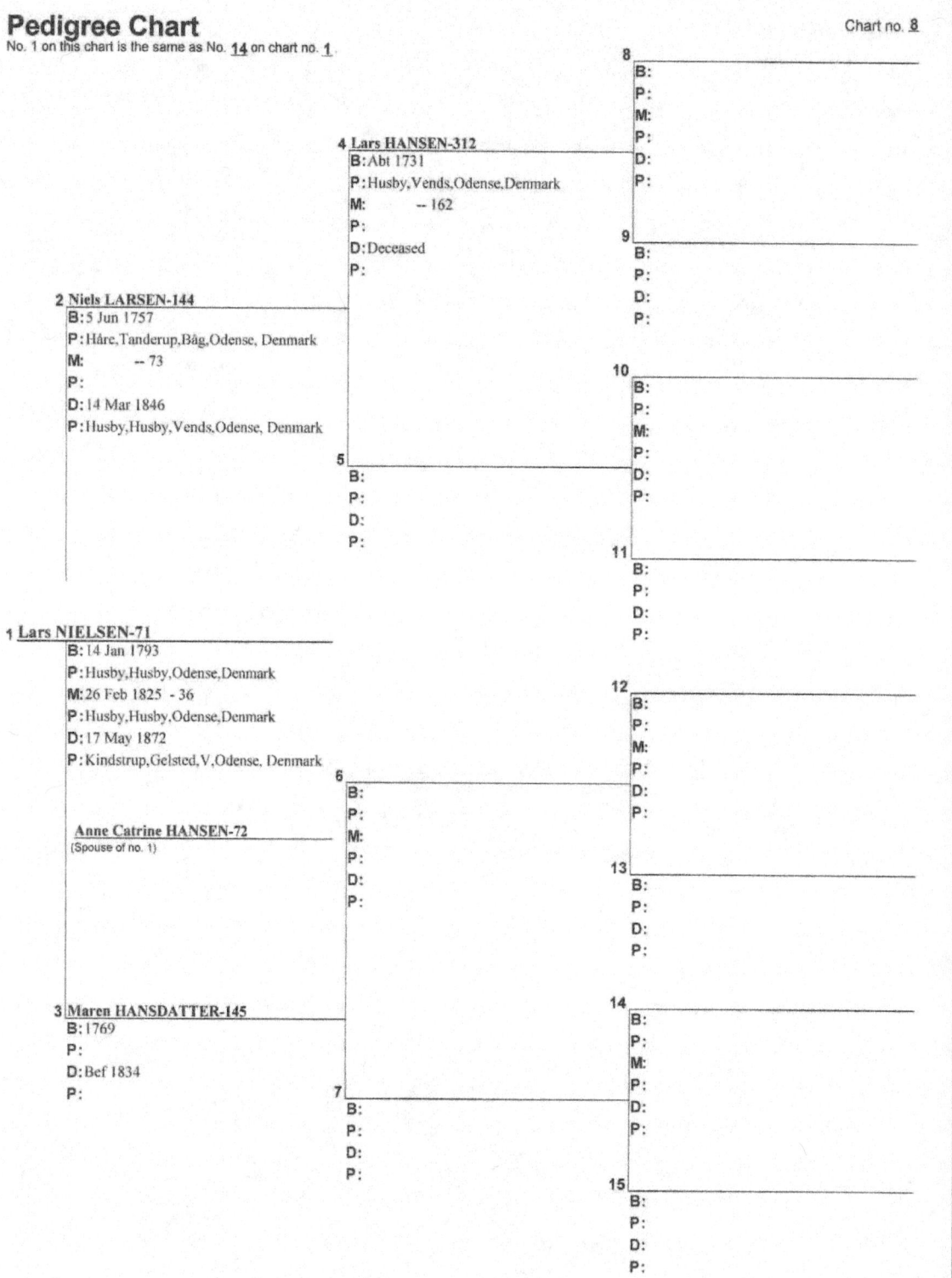

8
B:
P:
M:
P:
D:
P:

4 Lars HANSEN-312
B: Abt 1731
P: Husby,Vends,Odense,Denmark
M: -- 162
P:
D: Deceased
P:

9
B:
P:
D:
P:

2 Niels LARSEN-144
B: 5 Jun 1757
P: Håre,Tanderup,Båg,Odense, Denmark
M: -- 73
P:
D: 14 Mar 1846
P: Husby,Husby,Vends,Odense, Denmark

10
B:
P:
M:
P:
D:
P:

5
B:
P:
D:
P:

11
B:
P:
D:
P:

1 Lars NIELSEN-71
B: 14 Jan 1793
P: Husby,Husby,Odense,Denmark
M: 26 Feb 1825 - 36
P: Husby,Husby,Odense,Denmark
D: 17 May 1872
P: Kindstrup,Gelsted,V,Odense, Denmark

12
B:
P:
M:
P:
D:
P:

6
B:
P:
M:
P:
D:
P:

Anne Catrine HANSEN-72
(Spouse of no. 1)

13
B:
P:
D:
P:

3 Maren HANSDATTER-145
B: 1769
P:
D: Bef 1834
P:

14
B:
P:
M:
P:
D:
P:

7
B:
P:
D:
P:

15
B:
P:
D:
P:

Pedigree Chart

No. 1 on this chart is the same as No. 15 on chart no. 1.

8 Peder TERCHELSEN-588   66
B: 1675
P: Røjle,VS,VH,Odense Amt, Denmark
M: 27 Jun 1706 - 315
P: Vejlby Kirke,VS,V,Odense Amt, Denmark
D: 1740
P: Røjle,VS,VH,Odense Amt, Denmark

4 Soren PEDERSEN-313
B: 10 May 1722
P: Vejlby,Odense,Denmark
M: 12 Sep 1755 - 163
P: Rogle Molle,Vejlby,Odense,Denmark
D: 25 May 1798
P: Gelsted,Odense,Denmark

9 Bodil RASMUSDATTER-589
B: 1680
P:
D: Deceased
P:

2 Hans SORENSEN-146
R: 17 Jun 1759
P: Vejlby,Odense,Denmark
M: 29 Apr 1791 - 74
P: Kindstrup,Gelsted,Odense,Denmark
D: 26 Mar 1849
P: Kindstrup,Gelsted,Odense,Denmark

10 Hans ANDERSEN-590
B: Abt 1695
P:
M: -- 316
P:
D: Deceased
P:

5 Mette Sophie HANSEN-314
B: Abt 1720
P: Vejlby,Odense,Denmark
D: 13 Sep 1793
P: Kindstrup,Gelsted,Odense,Denmark

11 Maren POVELSEN-591   69
B: Abt 1694
P: Middelfart,Odense,Denmark
D: 19 Jun 1753
P: Vejlby,Odense,Denmark

1 Anne Catrine HANSEN-72
B: 27 Jun 1801
P: Kindstrup,Gelsted,Odense,Denmark
M: 26 Feb 1825 - 36
P: Husby,Husby,Odense,Denmark
D: 14 Jan 1841
P: Gelsted,Odense,Denmark

12 Lauritz MADSEN-592
B: 1705
P: Strandby,Ålborg,Denmark
M: 24 May 1744 - 317
P: Strandby,Aalborg,Denmark
D: Deceased
P:

6 Mads LAURITZSEN-315
B: Abt 1736
P: Gelsted,Odense,Denmark
M: 7 Apr 1762 - 164
P: Gamborg,Odense,Denmark
D: 19 Aug 1818
P: Gelsted,Odense,Denmark

Lars NIELSEN-71
(Spouse of no. 1)

13 Mette JENSEN-593   71
B: 7 Apr 1713
P: Ullits,Ålborg,Denmark
D: 11 Mar 1761
P: Ullits,Ålborg,Denmark

14 Mads PEDERSEN-594   72
B: 1693
P: Skaade,Aarhus,Denmark
M: 14 Nov 1728 - 318
P: Beder,Aarhus,Denmark
D: 23 Nov 1755
P: Skaade,Aarhus,Denmark

3 Kirsten MADSEN-147
B: 20 Nov 1768
P: Gelsted,Odense,Denmark
D: 19 Oct 1837
P: Gelsted,Odense,Denmark

7 Anne Catrine MADSDATTER-316
B: 1737
P: Skaade,Aarhus,Denmark
D: 7 Jun 1790
P: Gelsted,Odense,Denmark

15 Anne Cathrine RASMUSDATTER-595   73
B: 1700
P: Beder,Aarhus,Denmark
D: 28 Nov 1762
P:

Pedigree Chart

No. 1 on this chart is the same as No. **8** on chart no. **2**.

Chart no. **10**

74

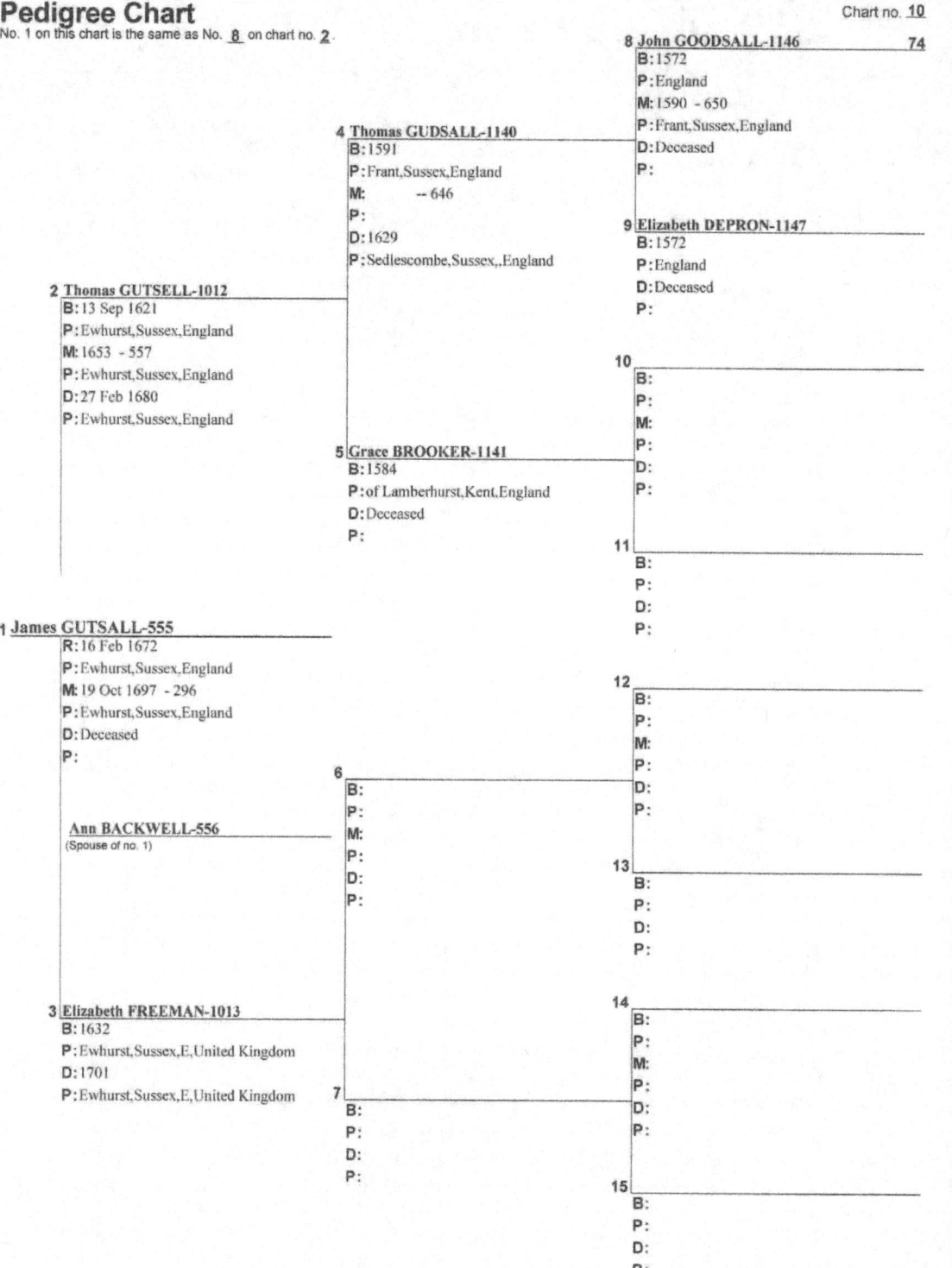

8 John GOODSALL-1146
B: 1572
P: England
M: 1590 – 650
P: Frant, Sussex, England
D: Deceased
P:

4 Thomas GUDSALL-1140
B: 1591
P: Frant, Sussex, England
M: -- 646
P:
D: 1629
P: Sedlescombe, Sussex,, England

9 Elizabeth DEPRON-1147
B: 1572
P: England
D: Deceased
P:

2 Thomas GUTSELL-1012
B: 13 Sep 1621
P: Ewhurst, Sussex, England
M: 1653 – 557
P: Ewhurst, Sussex, England
D: 27 Feb 1680
P: Ewhurst, Sussex, England

10
B:
P:
M:
P:
D:
P:

5 Grace BROOKER-1141
B: 1584
P: of Lamberhurst, Kent, England
D: Deceased
P:

11
B:
P:
D:
P:

1 James GUTSALL-555
R: 16 Feb 1672
P: Ewhurst, Sussex, England
M: 19 Oct 1697 – 296
P: Ewhurst, Sussex, England
D: Deceased
P:

12
B:
P:
M:
P:
D:
P:

6
B:
P:
M:
P:
D:
P:

13
B:
P:
D:
P:

Ann BACKWELL-556
(Spouse of no. 1)

14
B:
P:
M:
P:
D:
P:

3 Elizabeth FREEMAN-1013
B: 1632
P: Ewhurst, Sussex, E, United Kingdom
D: 1701
P: Ewhurst, Sussex, E, United Kingdom

7
B:
P:
D:
P:

15
B:
P:
D:
P:

Pedigree Chart

8 Humfrey BLACKWELL-1153
B: Abt 1570
P: England, United Kingdom
M: Abt 1590 - 654
P: England
D: Deceased
P:

4 Humfry BLACKWELL-1151
B: Abt 1600
P: Sussex, England, United Kingdom
M: 29 Sep 1617 - 653
P: Rudgwick, Sussex, England
D: Deceased
P:

9 Mrs. Blackwell -1154
B: Abt 1575
P: England, United Kingdom
D: Deceased
P:

2 Henry BLACKWELL-1015
R: 16 Sep 1632
P: Rudgwick, Sussex, England
M: 26 Nov 1668 - 559
P: Wadhurst, Sussex, England
D: Deceased
P:

10 John COMBER-1155   84
B: Abt 1572
P: Brighton, Sussex, England
M: 17 Oct 1591 - 655
P: St. Nicholas Parish, Brighton, S, England
D: Oct 1625
P: Brighton, Sussex, England

5 Agnis COMBER-1152
B: Abt 1600
P: England, United Kingdom
D: Deceased
P:

11 Leatyce GUNN-1156   85
R: 2 Apr 1570
P: Brighton, Sussex, England, United Kingdom
D: Deceased
P:

1 Ann BACKWELL-556
R: 7 May 1676
P: Ewhurst, Sussex, England
M: 19 Oct 1697 - 296
P: Ewhurst, Sussex, England
D: Deceased
P:

12 William LAKER-1195
B: 1585
P: Wadhurst, Sussex, England
M: Abt 1608 - 677
P: Sussex, England
D: Deceased
P:

6 Thomas LAKER-1193
B: Abt 1609
P: Wadhurst, Sussex, E, United Kingdom
M: 11 Aug 1634 - 676
P: Wadhurst, Sussex, England
D: Deceased
P:

James GUTSALL-555
(Spouse of no. 1)

13 Mrs. Mary LAKER-1196
B: 1585
P: Wadhurst, Sussex, England
D: Deceased
P:

14 HUES-1198
B: Abt 1585
P: England, United Kingdom
M: Abt 1610 - 679
P: England
D: Deceased
P:

3 Judith LAKER-1016
R: 11 Mar 1637
P: Wadhurst, Sussex, England
D: Deceased
P:

7 Judith HUES-1194
B: Abt 1613
P: Wadhurst, Sussex, E, United Kingdom
D: Deceased
P:

15 Mrs. Hues -1199
B: Abt 1590
P: England, United Kingdom
D: Deceased
P:

Pedigree Chart

No. 1 on this chart is the same as No. 8 on chart no. 3.

8 Richard BOOTES-1204   138
B: Abt 1550
P: Sussex,England,United Kingdom
M: Jun 1571 - 682
P: East Grinstead,Sussex,England
D: Deceased
P:

4 Richard BOOTES-1202
B: Abt 1578
P: Etchingham,Sussex,England
M: Abt 1603 - 681
P: Of Etchingham,Sussex,England
D: 30 May 1633
P: Sussex,England

9 Elizabeth ROLF-1205   139
B: Abt 1555
P: East Grinstead,Sussex,England
D: Deceased
P:

2 James BOOTES-1020
B: 10 May 1608
P: Etchingham,Sussex,England
M: 27 Oct 1634 - 562
P: Burwash,Sussex,England
D: 24 Oct 1667
P: Burwash,Sussex,England

10
B:
P:
M:
P:
D:
P:

5 Elinor -1203
B: Abt 1582
P: Etchingham,Sussex,E,United Kingdom
D: Deceased
P:

11
B:
P:
D:
P:

1 James BOOTES-565
B: 13 Jun 1645
P: Burwash,Sussex,E,United Kingdom
M: Abt 1698 - 302
P: Burwash,Sussex,England
D: 13 May 1705
P: Burwash,Sussex,England

12 Hugh WENAM-1212   142
B: 1550
P: Iden,Sussex,England,United Kingdom
M: 25 Jun 1571 - 686
P: Iden,Sussex,England
D: Deceased
P:

6 William WENHAM-1210
B: 23 Oct 1569
P: Iden,Sussex,England
M: 20 Jan 1608 - 685
P: Chalvington,Sussex,E,United Kingdom
D: Deceased
P:

13 Eve WILLES-1213   143
B: 1550
P: Iden,Sussex,England,United Kingdom
D: Deceased
P:

Susanna -566
(Spouse of no. 1)

14 Mr. SAINTGEORGE-1214
B: 1548
P: Chalvington,Sussex,England
M: -- 687
P:
D: Deceased
P: England

3 Anne WENHAM-1021
B: 2 Oct 1608
P: Chalvington,Sussex,England
D: 1681
P: Sussex,England,United Kingdom

7 Anne SAINTGEORGE-1211
B: 1570
P: Chalvington,Sussex,England
D: Deceased
P:

15 Mrs. SAINTGEORGE-1215
B: 1548
P: Chalvington,Sussex,England
D: Deceased
P: England

06 Nov 2015

Pedigree Chart

No. 1 on this chart is the same as No. **10** on chart no. **3**.

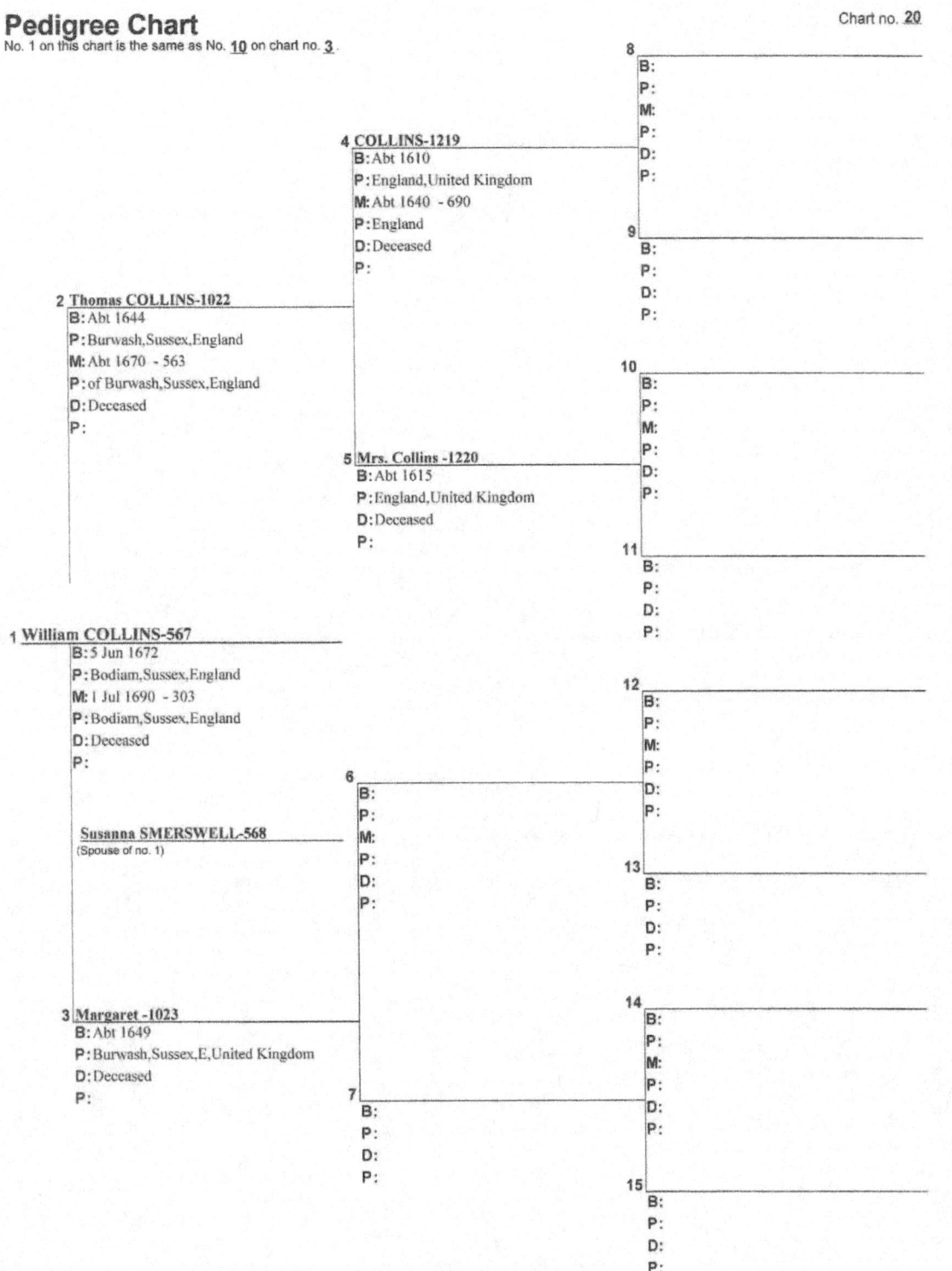

8
B:
P:
M:
P:
D:
P:

4 COLLINS-1219
B: Abt 1610
P: England, United Kingdom
M: Abt 1640 - 690
P: England
D: Deceased
P:

9
B:
P:
D:
P:

2 Thomas COLLINS-1022
B: Abt 1644
P: Burwash, Sussex, England
M: Abt 1670 - 563
P: of Burwash, Sussex, England
D: Deceased
P:

5 Mrs. Collins -1220
B: Abt 1615
P: England, United Kingdom
D: Deceased
P:

10
B:
P:
M:
P:
D:
P:

11
B:
P:
D:
P:

1 William COLLINS-567
B: 5 Jun 1672
P: Bodiam, Sussex, England
M: 1 Jul 1690 - 303
P: Bodiam, Sussex, England
D: Deceased
P:

6
B:
P:
M:
P:
D:
P:

12
B:
P:
M:
P:
D:
P:

13
B:
P:
D:
P:

Susanna SMERSWELL-568
(Spouse of no. 1)

3 Margaret -1023
B: Abt 1649
P: Burwash, Sussex, E, United Kingdom
D: Deceased
P:

7
B:
P:
D:
P:

14
B:
P:
M:
P:
D:
P:

15
B:
P:
D:
P:

Pedigree Chart

No. 1 on this chart is the same as No. **11** on chart no. **3**.

8 John SMERSALL-1223   **162**
B: Abt 1568
P: Brede,Sussex,England,United Kingdom
M: 11 Jun 1593 - 692
P: Brede,Sussex,England
D: Deceased
P:

4 John SMERSALL the Third-1221
B: Abt 1604
P: Bodiam,Sussex,E,United Kingdom
M: 7 Aug 1629 - 691
P: Bodiam,Sussex,England
D: Deceased
P:

9 Margaret CHESMAN-1224   **163**
B: 1575
P: Brede,Sussex,England,United Kingdom
D: Deceased
P:

2 William SMERSWELL-1024
B: Abt 1630
P: Bodiam,Sussex,E,United Kingdom
M: 22 Oct 1654 - 564
P: Bodiam,Sussex,England
D: Deceased
P:

10 Robert BOURNE-1225   **164**
B: Abt 1570
P: Bodiam,Sussex,England,United Kingdom
M: Abt 1593 - 693
P: Bodian,,Sussex,England
D: 28 Feb 1605
P: England,United Kingdom

5 Dorothy BOORNE OR BOURNE-1222
B: Abt 1608
P: Bodiam,Sussex,E,United Kingdom
D: Deceased
P:

11 Susan MOORE-1226   **165**
B: Abt 1574
P: Rye,Sussex,England,United Kingdom
D: 29 Jan 1645
P:

1 Susanna SMERSWELL-568
B: 1661
P: Bodiam,Sussex,E,United Kingdom
M: 1 Jul 1690 - 303
P: Bodiam,Sussex,England
D: Deceased
P:

12
B:
P:
M:
P:
D:
P:

6 BAKER-1266
B: Abt 1600
P: England,United Kingdom
M: Abt 1630 - 726
P: England
D: Deceased
P:

13
B:
P:
D:
P:

William COLLINS-567
(Spouse of no. 1)

3 Ann BAKER-1025
B: Abt 1633
P: Bodiam,Sussex,E,United Kingdom
D: Deceased
P:

14
B:
P:
M:
P:
D:
P:

7 Mrs. Baker -1267
B: Abt 1603
P: England,United Kingdom
D: Deceased
P:

15
B:
P:
D:
P:

06 Nov 2015

Pedigree Chart

No. 1 on this chart is the same as No. _9_ on chart no. _4_.

Chart no. _27_

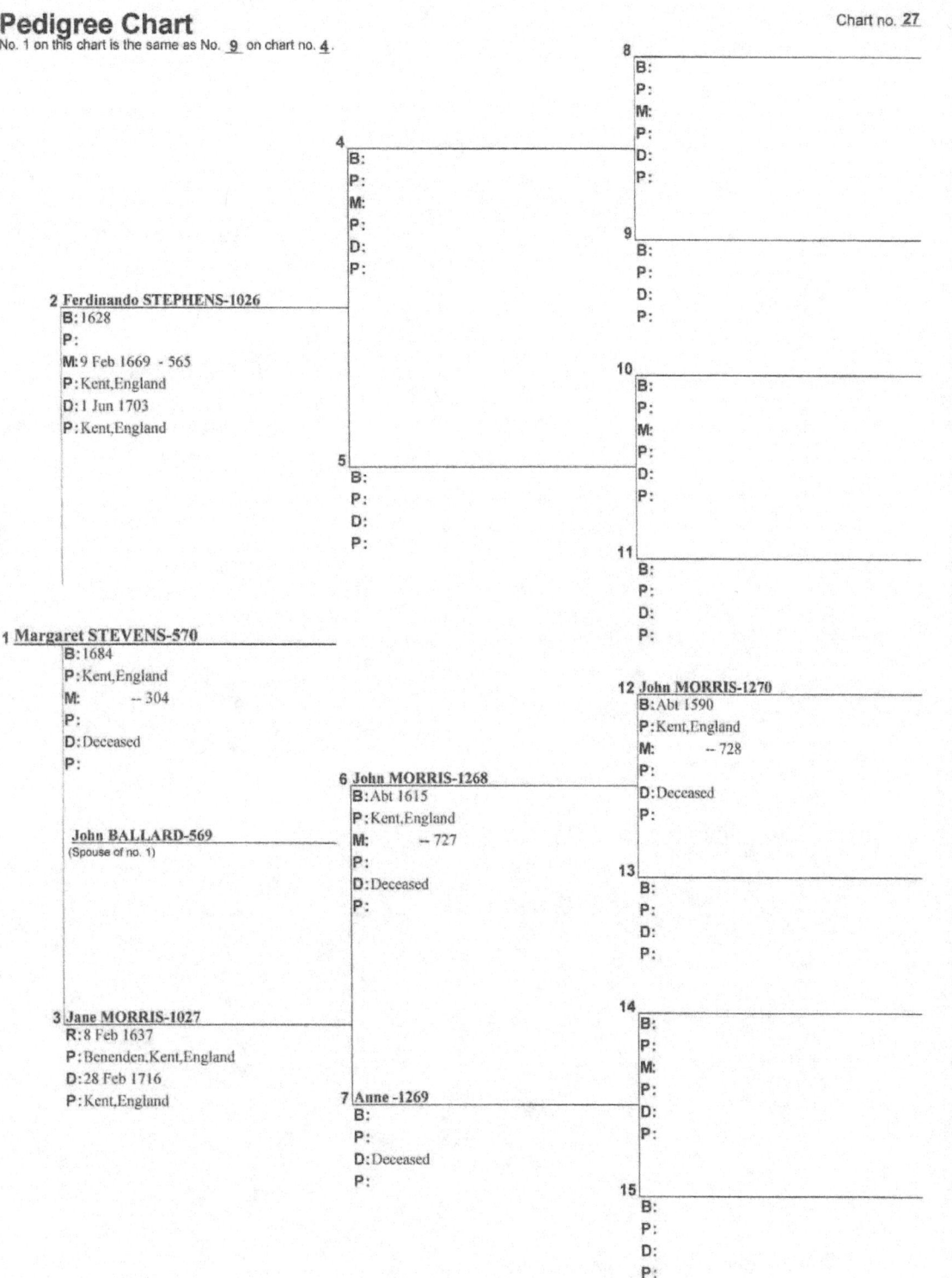

8
B:
P:
M:
P:
D:
P:

4
B:
P:
M:
P:
D:
P:

9
B:
P:
D:
P:

2 **Ferdinando STEPHENS-1026**
B: 1628
P:
M: 9 Feb 1669 - 565
P: Kent,England
D: 1 Jun 1703
P: Kent,England

10
B:
P:
M:
P:
D:
P:

5
B:
P:
D:
P:

11
B:
P:
D:
P:

1 **Margaret STEVENS-570**
B: 1684
P: Kent,England
M: -- 304
P:
D: Deceased
P:

12 **John MORRIS-1270**
B: Abt 1590
P: Kent,England
M: -- 728
P:
D: Deceased
P:

6 **John MORRIS-1268**
B: Abt 1615
P: Kent,England
M: -- 727
P:
D: Deceased
P:

John BALLARD-569
(Spouse of no. 1)

13
B:
P:
D:
P:

3 **Jane MORRIS-1027**
R: 8 Feb 1637
P: Benenden,Kent,England
D: 28 Feb 1716
P: Kent,England

14
B:
P:
M:
P:
D:
P:

7 **Anne -1269**
B:
P:
D: Deceased
P:

15
B:
P:
D:
P:

06 Nov 2015

Pedigree Chart

No. 1 on this chart is the same as No. _8_ on chart no. _5_.

Chart no. _34_

8 William HOBDEN-1273   266
B: 1597
P: Sussex, England
M: 21 Nov 1621 - 730
P: Crowhurst, Sussex, England
D:
P: England

4 Thomas HOBDEN-1271
B: Abt 1634
P: Hamsey, Sussex, E, United Kingdom
M: 19 May 1663 - 729
P: Hamsey, Sussex, England
D: Deceased
P:

9 Agnes GEERAT-1274
B:
P:
D:
P: England

2 William HOBDEN-1028
B: 4 Mar 1664
P: Chailey, Barcombe, Sussex, England
M: 29 May 1696 - 567
P:
D: 25 May 1734
P: Sussex, England

10 John PARKER-1275
B: 3 May 1617
P: Erwarton, Suffolk, E, United Kingdom
M: 1638 - 731
P: England
D: Deceased
P:

5 Jane PARKER-1272
B: 1639
P: England
D: 1728
P: Sussex, England

11 Judith TREE-1276
B: 1617
P: Sussex, England
D:
P: Sussex, England

1 Thomas HOBDEN-571
B: 1700
P: Sussex, England, United Kingdom
M: 5 Dec 1725 - 305
P: St Ann, Lewes, Sussex, England
D: 16 Jan 1768
P: Maresfield, Sussex, England

12
B:
P:
M:
P:
D:
P:

6 John BRIGHTRIDGE-1293
B: Abt 1648
P: Barcombe, Sussex, England
M: Abt 1666 - 744
P: Barcombe, Sussex, England
D: Deceased
P:

Catherine HUMPHREY-572
(Spouse of no. 1)

13
B:
P:
D:
P:

3 Mary BRIGHTRIDGE-1029
B: Abt 1668
P: Barcombe, Sussex, England
D: 3 Jun 1712
P: Sussex, England

14
B:
P:
M:
P:
D:
P:

7 Ellinor CARMAN-1294
B: Abt 1652
P: Barcombe, Sussex, England
D: Deceased
P:

15
B:
P:
D:
P:

Pedigree Chart

No. 1 on this chart is the same as No. 11 on chart no. 5.

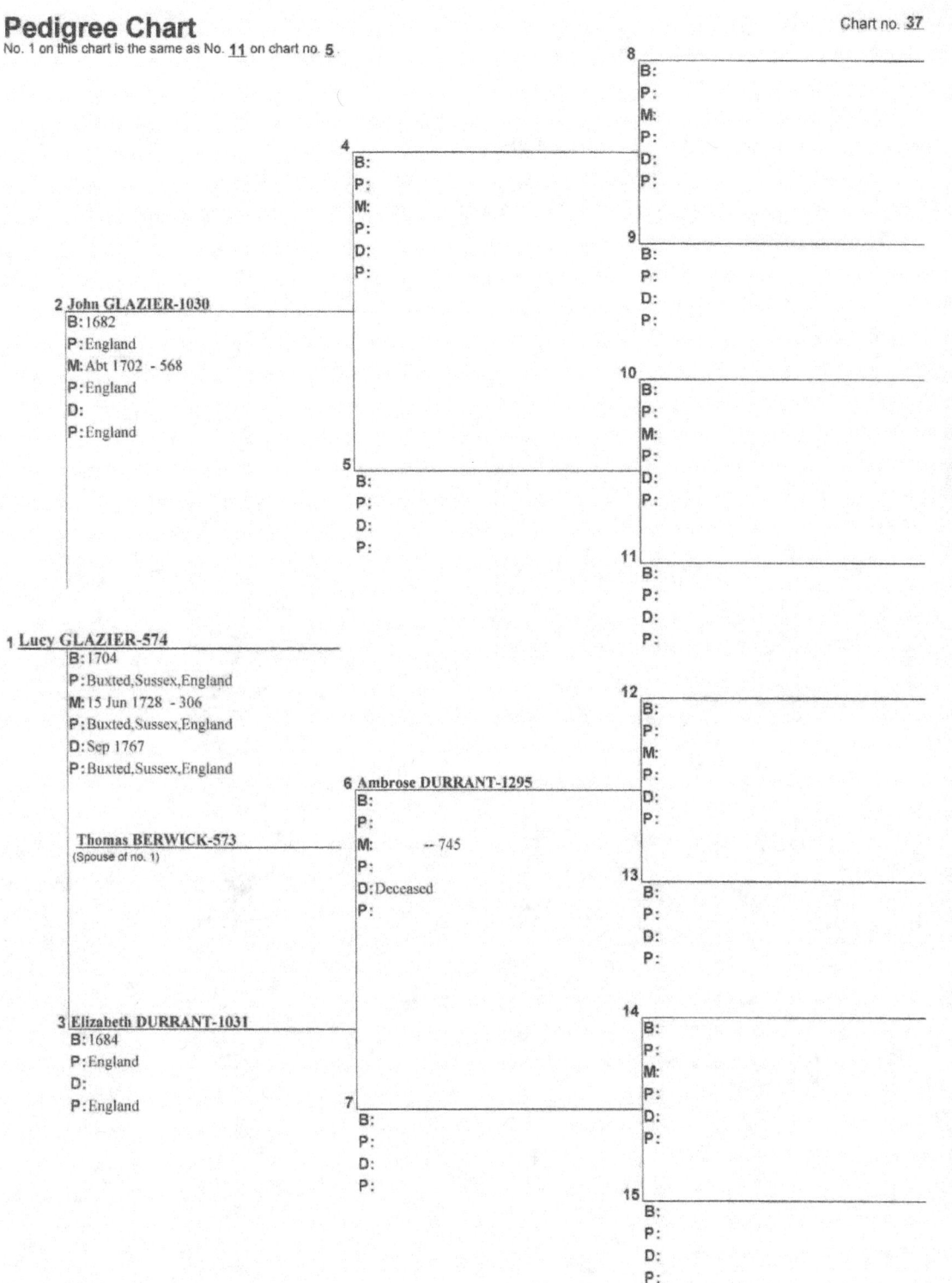

8
B:
P:
M:
P:
D:
P:

4
B:
P:
M:
P:
D:
P:

9
B:
P:
D:
P:

2 John GLAZIER-1030
B: 1682
P: England
M: Abt 1702 - 568
P: England
D:
P: England

10
B:
P:
M:
P:
D:
P:

5
B:
P:
D:
P:

11
B:
P:
D:
P:

1 Lucy GLAZIER-574
B: 1704
P: Buxted,Sussex,England
M: 15 Jun 1728 - 306
P: Buxted,Sussex,England
D: Sep 1767
P: Buxted,Sussex,England

12
B:
P:
M:
P:
D:
P:

6 Ambrose DURRANT-1295
B:
P:
M: -- 745
P:
D: Deceased
P:

Thomas BERWICK-573
(Spouse of no. 1)

13
B:
P:
D:
P:

3 Elizabeth DURRANT-1031
B: 1684
P: England
D:
P: England

14
B:
P:
M:
P:
D:
P:

7
B:
P:
D:
P:

15
B:
P:
D:
P:

06 Nov 2015

No. 1 on this chart is the same as No. **8** on chart no. **9** .

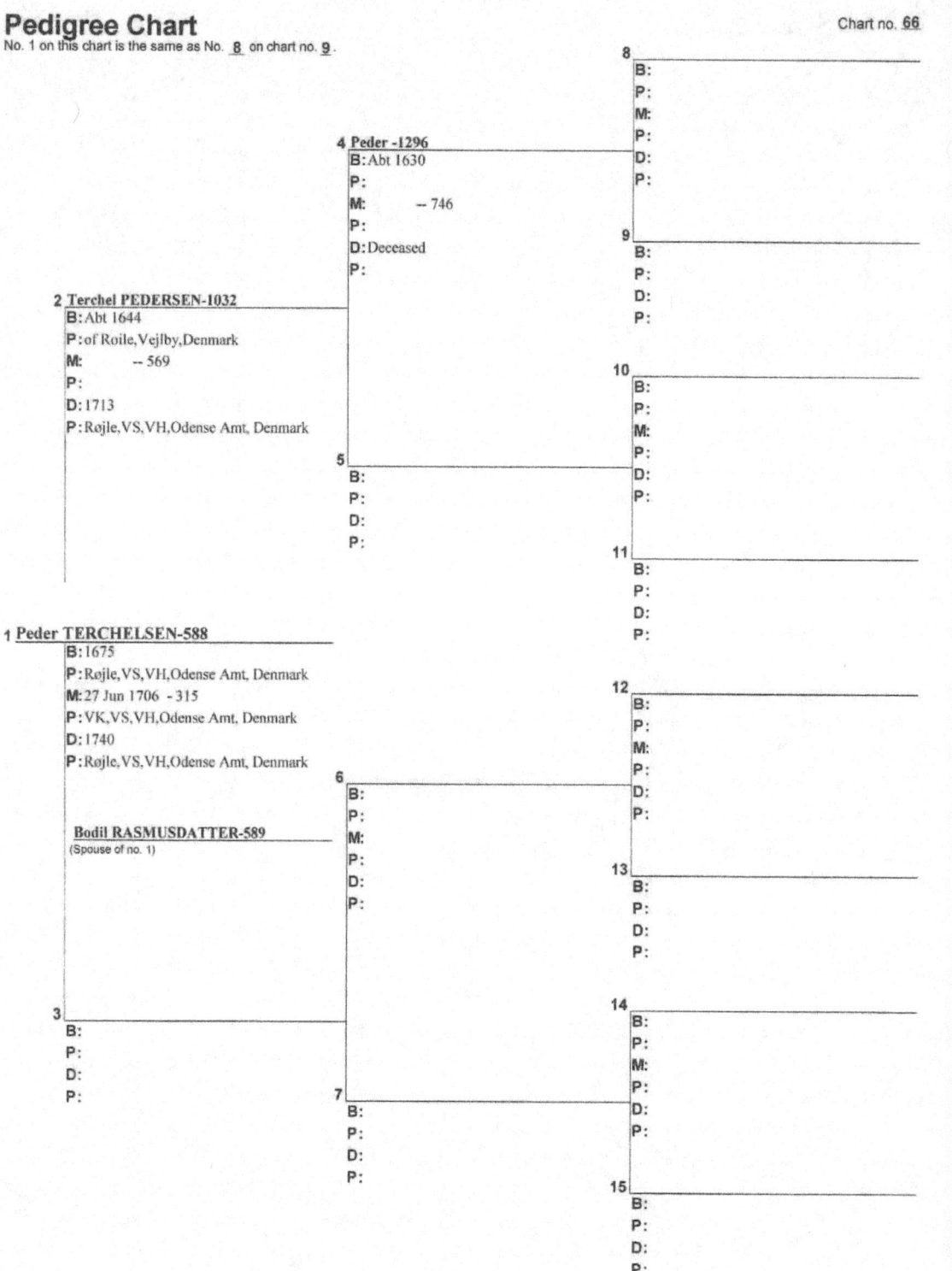

4 Peder -1296
B: Abt 1630
P:
M: -- 746
P:
D: Deceased
P:

2 Terchel PEDERSEN-1032
B: Abt 1644
P: of Roile, Vejlby, Denmark
M: -- 569
P:
D: 1713
P: Røjle, VS, VH, Odense Amt, Denmark

5
B:
P:
D:
P:

1 Peder TERCHELSEN-588
B: 1675
P: Røjle, VS, VH, Odense Amt, Denmark
M: 27 Jun 1706 - 315
P: VK, VS, VH, Odense Amt, Denmark
D: 1740
P: Røjle, VS, VH, Odense Amt, Denmark

Bodil RASMUSDATTER-589
(Spouse of no. 1)

3
B:
P:
D:
P:

6
B:
P:
M:
P:
D:
P:

7
B:
P:
D:
P:

8
B:
P:
M:
P:
D:
P:

9
B:
P:
D:
P:

10
B:
P:
M:
P:
D:
P:

11
B:
P:
D:
P:

12
B:
P:
M:
P:
D:
P:

13
B:
P:
D:
P:

14
B:
P:
M:
P:
D:
P:

15
B:
P:
D:
P:

06 Nov 2015

Pedigree Chart

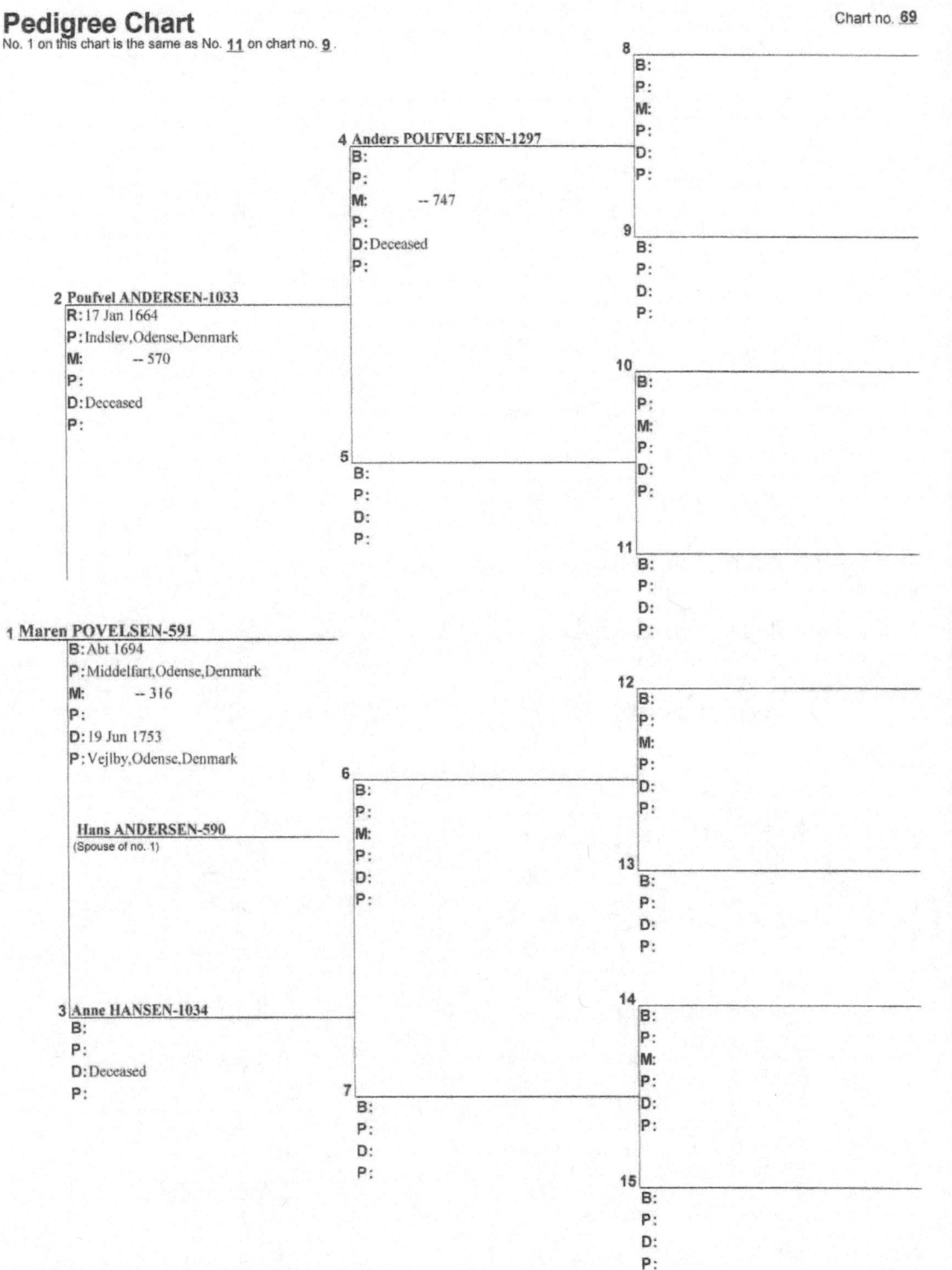

8
B:
P:
M:
P:
D:
P:

4 Anders POUFVELSEN-1297
B:
P:
M: -- 747
P:
D: Deceased
P:

9
B:
P:
D:
P:

2 Poufvel ANDERSEN-1033
R: 17 Jan 1664
P: Indslev,Odense,Denmark
M: -- 570
P:
D: Deceased
P:

10
B:
P:
M:
P:
D:
P:

5
B:
P:
D:
P:

11
B:
P:
D:
P:

1 Maren POVELSEN-591
B: Abt 1694
P: Middelfart,Odense,Denmark
M: -- 316
P:
D: 19 Jun 1753
P: Vejlby,Odense,Denmark

12
B:
P:
M:
P:
D:
P:

6
B:
P:
M:
P:
D:
P:

Hans ANDERSEN-590
(Spouse of no. 1)

13
B:
P:
D:
P:

3 Anne HANSEN-1034
B:
P:
D: Deceased
P:

14
B:
P:
M:
P:
D:
P:

7
B:
P:
D:
P:

15
B:
P:
D:
P:

06 Nov 2015

No. 1 on this chart is the same as No. 13 on chart no. 9 .

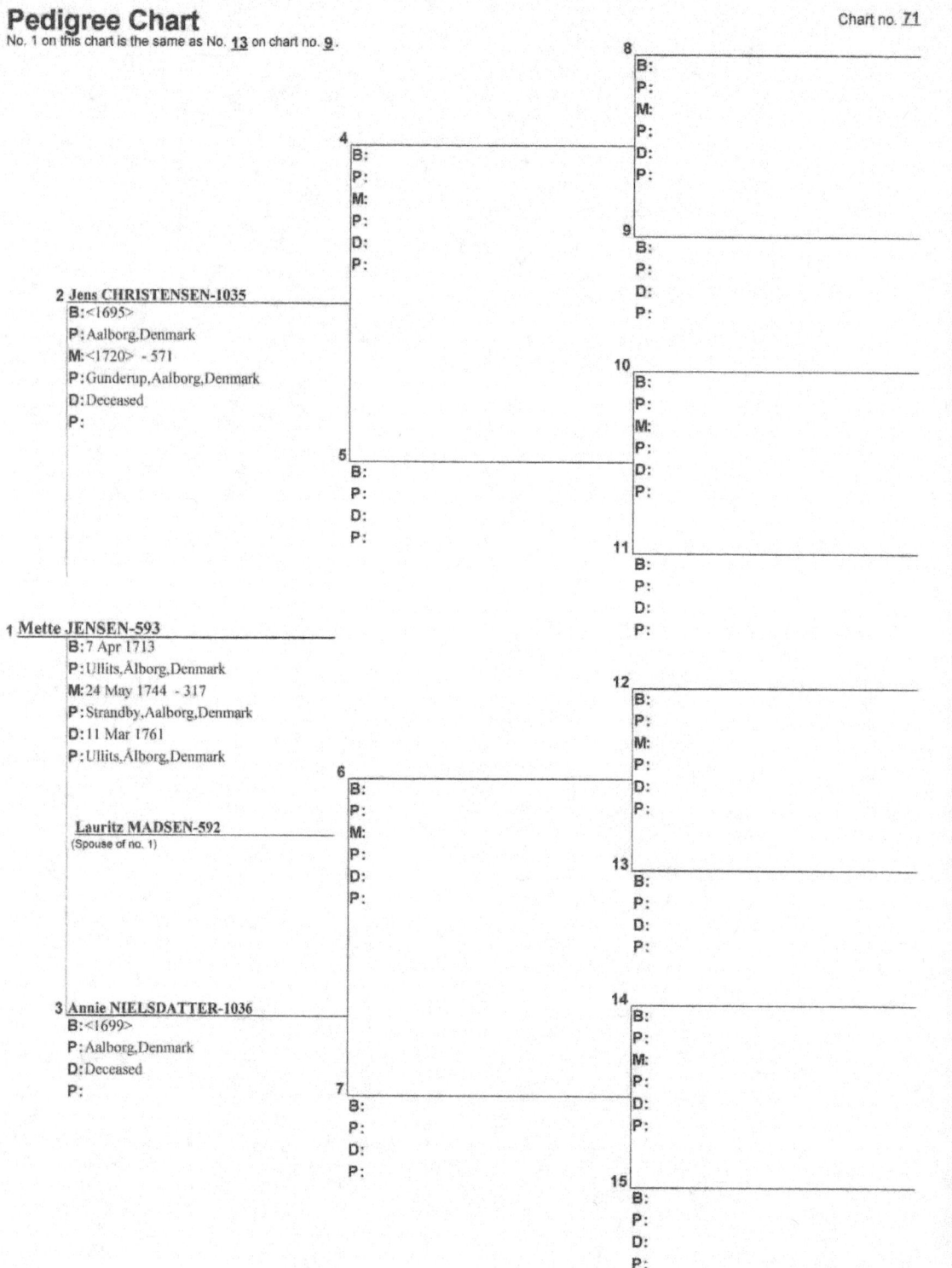

2 Jens CHRISTENSEN-1035
B: <1695>
P: Aalborg,Denmark
M: <1720> - 571
P: Gunderup,Aalborg,Denmark
D: Deceased
P:

1 Mette JENSEN-593
B: 7 Apr 1713
P: Ullits,Ålborg,Denmark
M: 24 May 1744 - 317
P: Strandby,Aalborg,Denmark
D: 11 Mar 1761
P: Ullits,Ålborg,Denmark

Lauritz MADSEN-592
(Spouse of no. 1)

3 Annie NIELSDATTER-1036
B: <1699>
P: Aalborg,Denmark
D: Deceased
P:

4
B:
P:
M:
P:
D:
P:

5
B:
P:
D:
P:

6
B:
P:
M:
P:
D:
P:

7
B:
P:
D:
P:

8
B:
P:
M:
P:
D:
P:

9
B:
P:
D:
P:

10
B:
P:
M:
P:
D:
P:

11
B:
P:
D:
P:

12
B:
P:
M:
P:
D:
P:

13
B:
P:
D:
P:

14
B:
P:
M:
P:
D:
P:

15
B:
P:
D:
P:

06 Nov 2015

Pedigree Chart

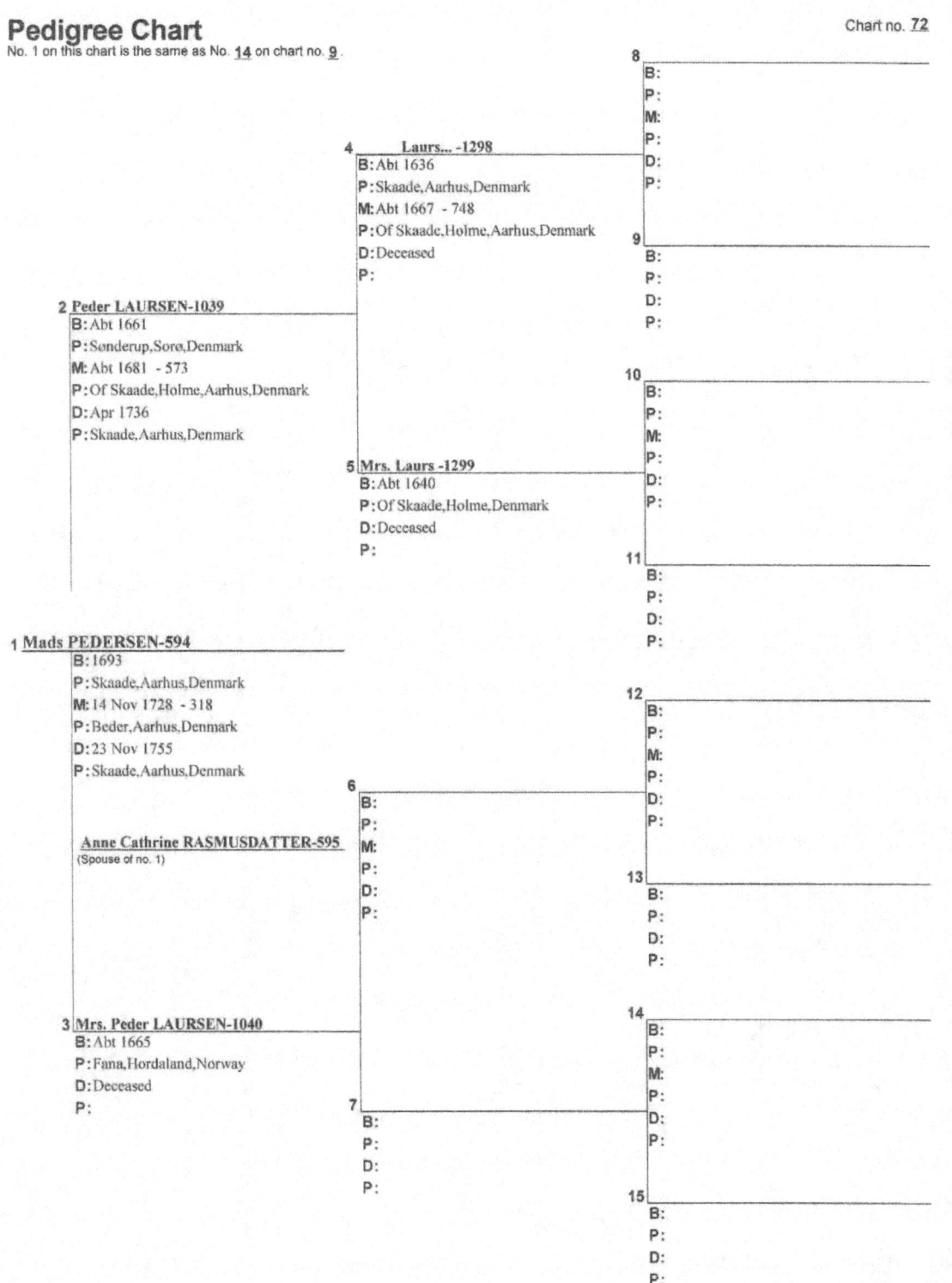

8
B:
P:
M:
P:
D:
P:

4 Laurs... -1298
B: Abt 1636
P: Skaade, Aarhus, Denmark
M: Abt 1667 - 748
P: Of Skaade, Holme, Aarhus, Denmark
D: Deceased
P:

9
B:
P:
D:
P:

2 Peder LAURSEN-1039
B: Abt 1661
P: Sønderup, Sorø, Denmark
M: Abt 1681 - 573
P: Of Skaade, Holme, Aarhus, Denmark
D: Apr 1736
P: Skaade, Aarhus, Denmark

10
B:
P:
M:
P:
D:
P:

5 Mrs. Laurs -1299
B: Abt 1640
P: Of Skaade, Holme, Denmark
D: Deceased
P:

11
B:
P:
D:
P:

1 Mads PEDERSEN-594
B: 1693
P: Skaade, Aarhus, Denmark
M: 14 Nov 1728 - 318
P: Beder, Aarhus, Denmark
D: 23 Nov 1755
P: Skaade, Aarhus, Denmark

12
B:
P:
M:
P:
D:
P:

6
B:
P:
M:
P:
D:
P:

13
B:
P:
D:
P:

Anne Cathrine RASMUSDATTER-595
(Spouse of no. 1)

14
B:
P:
M:
P:
D:
P:

3 Mrs. Peder LAURSEN-1040
B: Abt 1665
P: Fana, Hordaland, Norway
D: Deceased
P:

7
B:
P:
D:
P:

15
B:
P:
D:
P:

06 Nov 2015

No. 1 on this chart is the same as No. <u>15</u> on chart no. <u>9</u>.

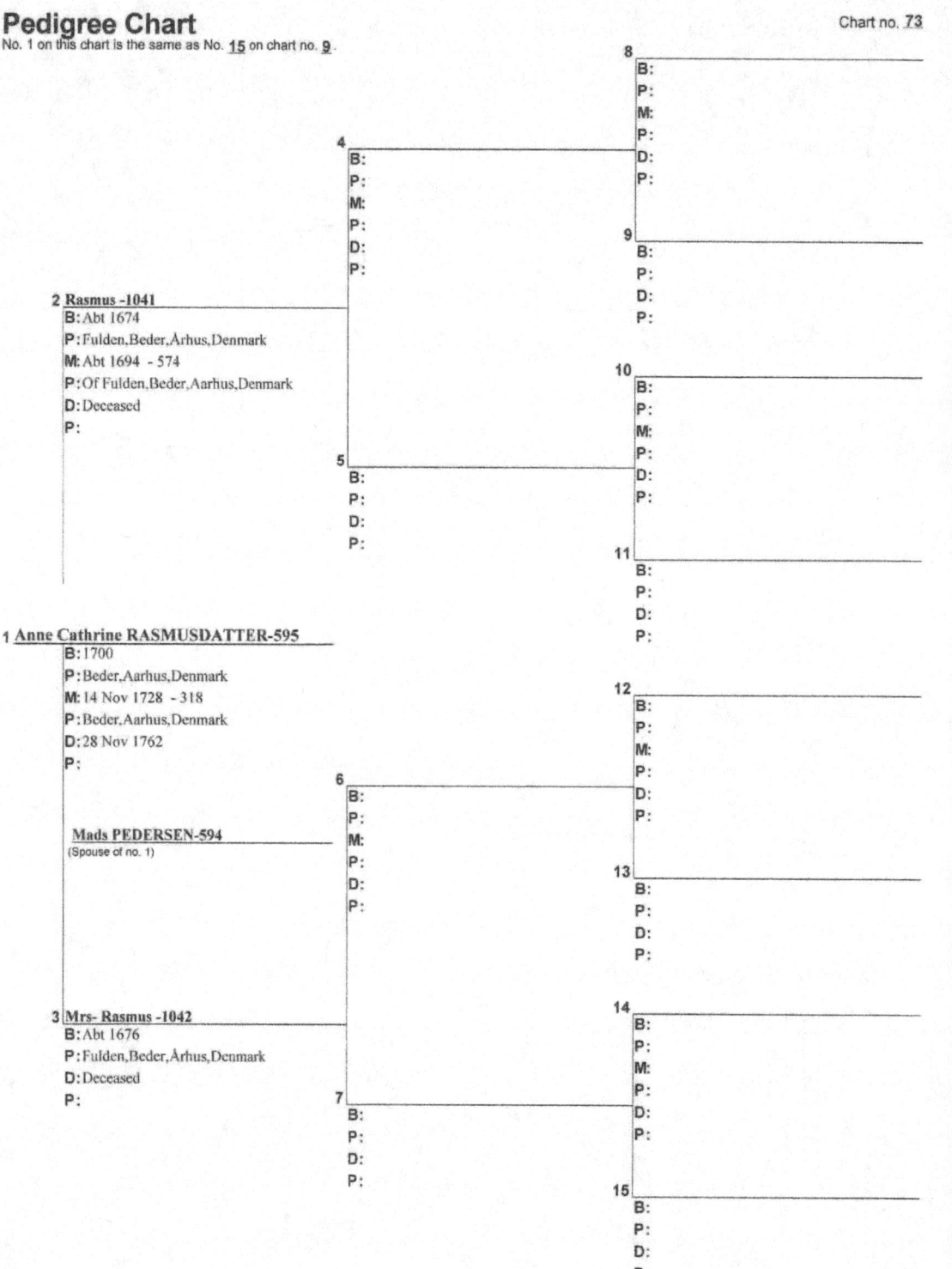

8
B:
P:
M:
P:
D:
P:

4
B:
P:
M:
P:
D:
P:

9
B:
P:
D:
P:

2 Rasmus -1041
B: Abt 1674
P: Fulden,Beder,Århus,Denmark
M: Abt 1694 - 574
P: Of Fulden,Beder,Aarhus,Denmark
D: Deceased
P:

10
B:
P:
M:
P:
D:
P:

5
B:
P:
D:
P:

11
B:
P:
D:
P:

1 Anne Cathrine RASMUSDATTER-595
B: 1700
P: Beder,Aarhus,Denmark
M: 14 Nov 1728 - 318
P: Beder,Aarhus,Denmark
D: 28 Nov 1762
P:

12
B:
P:
M:
P:
D:
P:

6
B:
P:
M:
P:
D:
P:

Mads PEDERSEN-594
(Spouse of no. 1)

13
B:
P:
D:
P:

3 Mrs- Rasmus -1042
B: Abt 1676
P: Fulden,Beder,Århus,Denmark
D: Deceased
P:

14
B:
P:
M:
P:
D:
P:

7
B:
P:
D:
P:

15
B:
P:
D:
P:

Pedigree Chart

No. 1 on this chart is the same as No. _8_ on chart no. _10_ .

Chart no. _74_

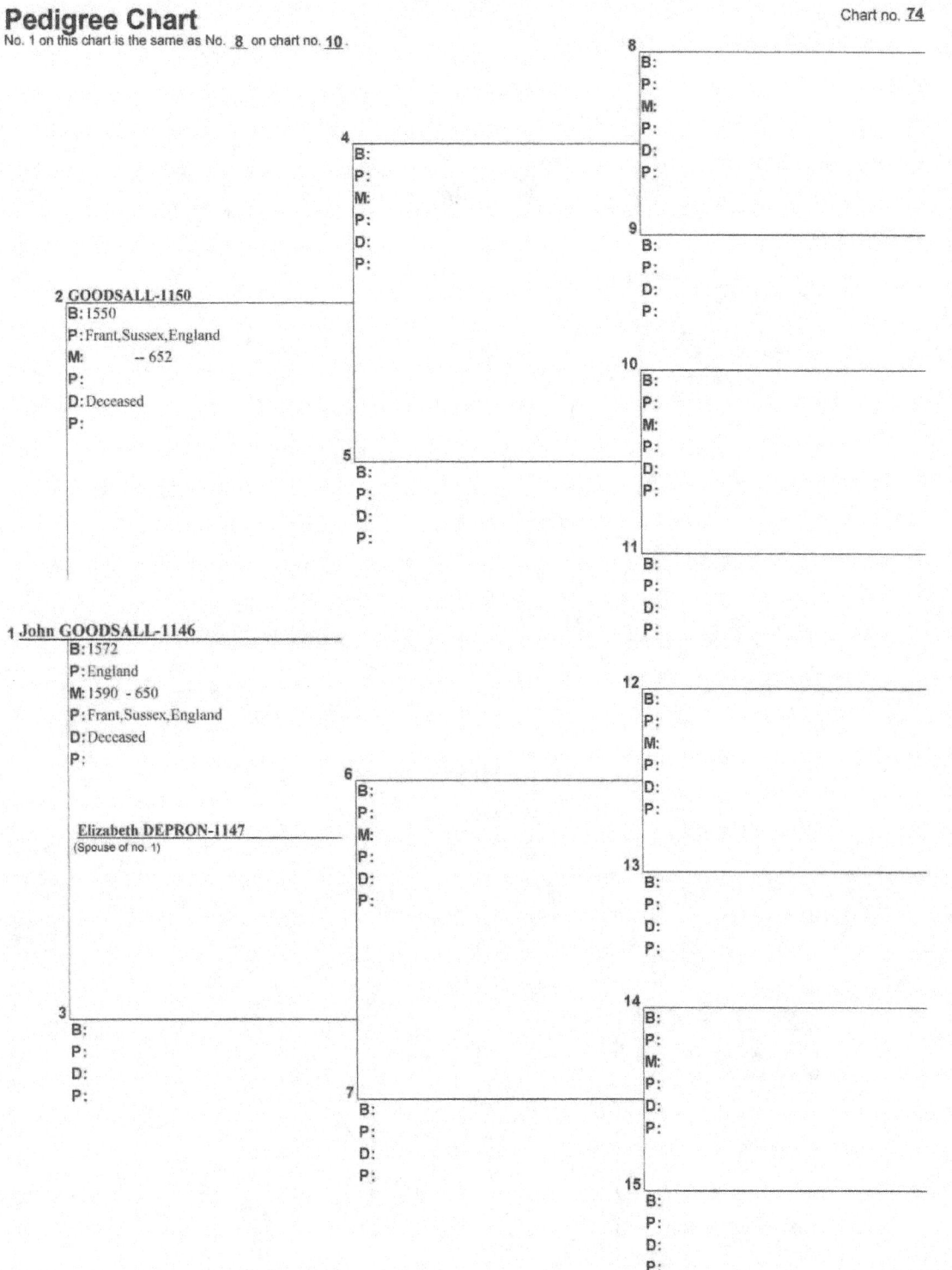

8
B:
P:
M:
P:
D:
P:

4
B:
P:
M:
P:
D:
P:

9
B:
P:
D:
P:

2 GOODSALL-1150
B: 1550
P: Frant,Sussex,England
M: -- 652
P:
D: Deceased
P:

10
B:
P:
M:
P:
D:
P:

5
B:
P:
D:
P:

11
B:
P:
D:
P:

1 John GOODSALL-1146
B: 1572
P: England
M: 1590 - 650
P: Frant,Sussex,England
D: Deceased
P:

12
B:
P:
M:
P:
D:
P:

6
B:
P:
M:
P:
D:
P:

Elizabeth DEPRON-1147
(Spouse of no. 1)

13
B:
P:
D:
P:

3
B:
P:
D:
P:

14
B:
P:
M:
P:
D:
P:

7
B:
P:
D:
P:

15
B:
P:
D:
P:

06 Nov 2015

Pedigree Chart

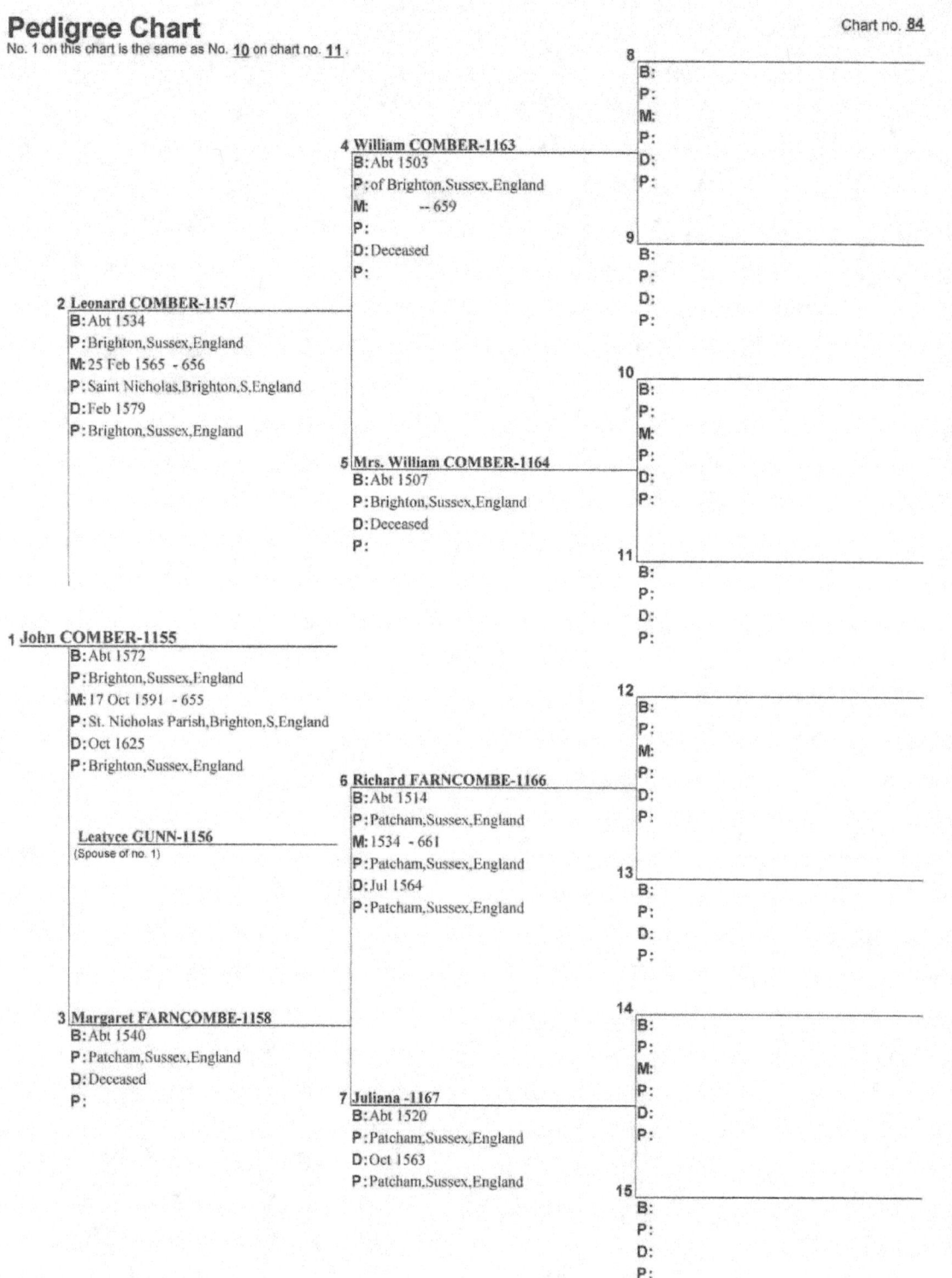

4 William COMBER-1163
B: Abt 1503
P: of Brighton,Sussex,England
M: -- 659
P:
D: Deceased
P:

2 Leonard COMBER-1157
B: Abt 1534
P: Brighton,Sussex,England
M: 25 Feb 1565 - 656
P: Saint Nicholas,Brighton,S,England
D: Feb 1579
P: Brighton,Sussex,England

5 Mrs. William COMBER-1164
B: Abt 1507
P: Brighton,Sussex,England
D: Deceased
P:

1 John COMBER-1155
B: Abt 1572
P: Brighton,Sussex,England
M: 17 Oct 1591 - 655
P: St. Nicholas Parish,Brighton,S,England
D: Oct 1625
P: Brighton,Sussex,England

Leatyce GUNN-1156
(Spouse of no. 1)

6 Richard FARNCOMBE-1166
B: Abt 1514
P: Patcham,Sussex,England
M: 1534 - 661
P: Patcham,Sussex,England
D: Jul 1564
P: Patcham,Sussex,England

3 Margaret FARNCOMBE-1158
B: Abt 1540
P: Patcham,Sussex,England
D: Deceased
P:

7 Juliana -1167
B: Abt 1520
P: Patcham,Sussex,England
D: Oct 1563
P: Patcham,Sussex,England

8
B:
P:
M:
P:
D:
P:

9
B:
P:
D:
P:

10
B:
P:
M:
P:
D:
P:

11
B:
P:
D:
P:

12
B:
P:
M:
P:
D:
P:

13
B:
P:
D:
P:

14
B:
P:
M:
P:
D:
P:

15
B:
P:
D:
P:

Pedigree Chart

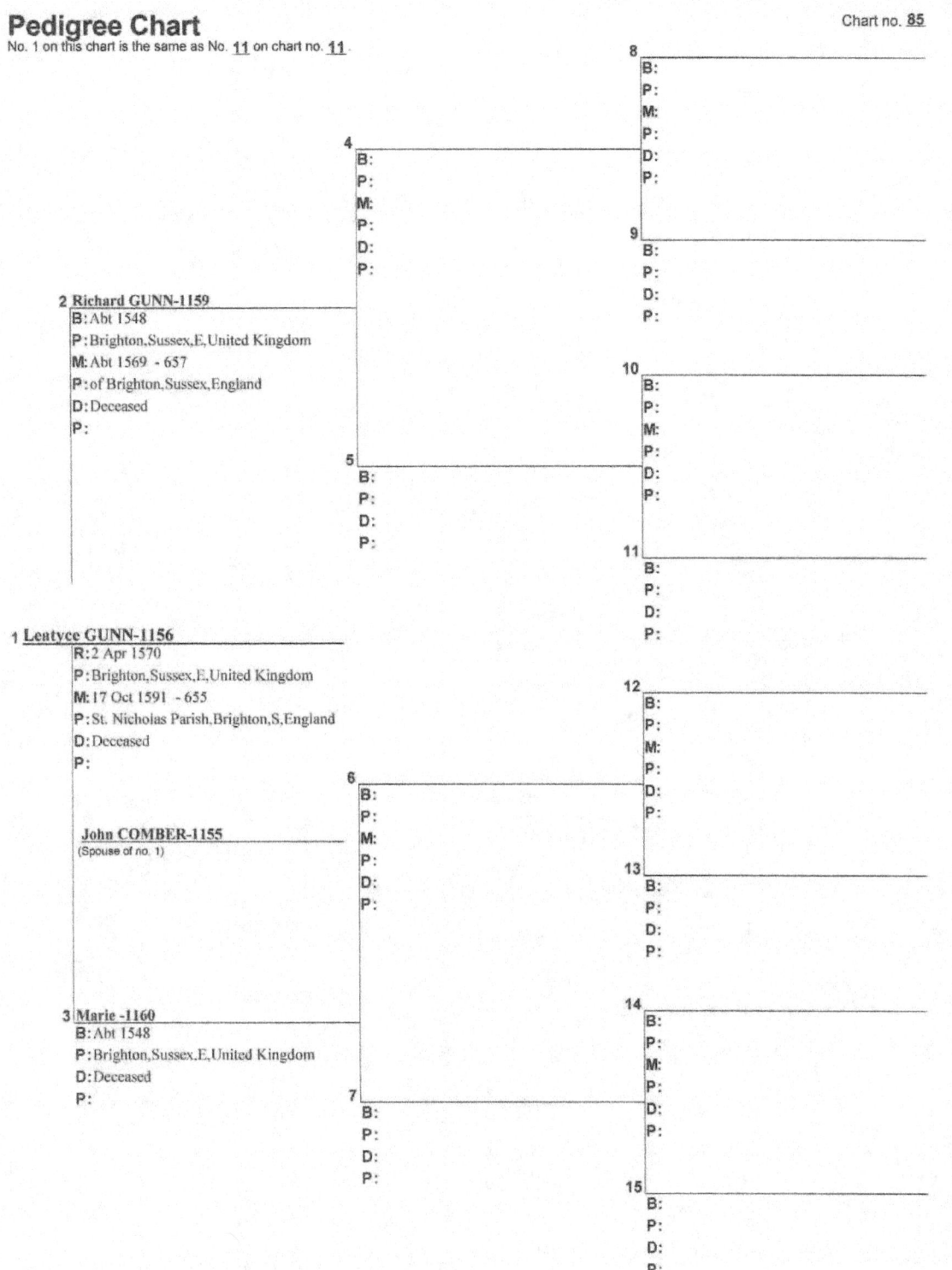

8
B:
P:
M:
P:
D:
P:

4
B:
P:
M:
P:
D:
P:

9
B:
P:
D:
P:

2 Richard GUNN-1159
B: Abt 1548
P: Brighton,Sussex,E,United Kingdom
M: Abt 1569 - 657
P: of Brighton,Sussex,England
D: Deceased
P:

10
B:
P:
M:
P:
D:
P:

5
B:
P:
D:
P:

11
B:
P:
D:
P:

1 Lentyce GUNN-1156
R: 2 Apr 1570
P: Brighton,Sussex,E,United Kingdom
M: 17 Oct 1591 - 655
P: St. Nicholas Parish,Brighton,S,England
D: Deceased
P:

12
B:
P:
M:
P:
D:
P:

John COMBER-1155
(Spouse of no. 1)

6
B:
P:
M:
P:
D:
P:

13
B:
P:
D:
P:

3 Marie -1160
B: Abt 1548
P: Brighton,Sussex,E,United Kingdom
D: Deceased
P:

14
B:
P:
M:
P:
D:
P:

7
B:
P:
D:
P:

15
B:
P:
D:
P:

06 Nov 2015

Pedigree Chart

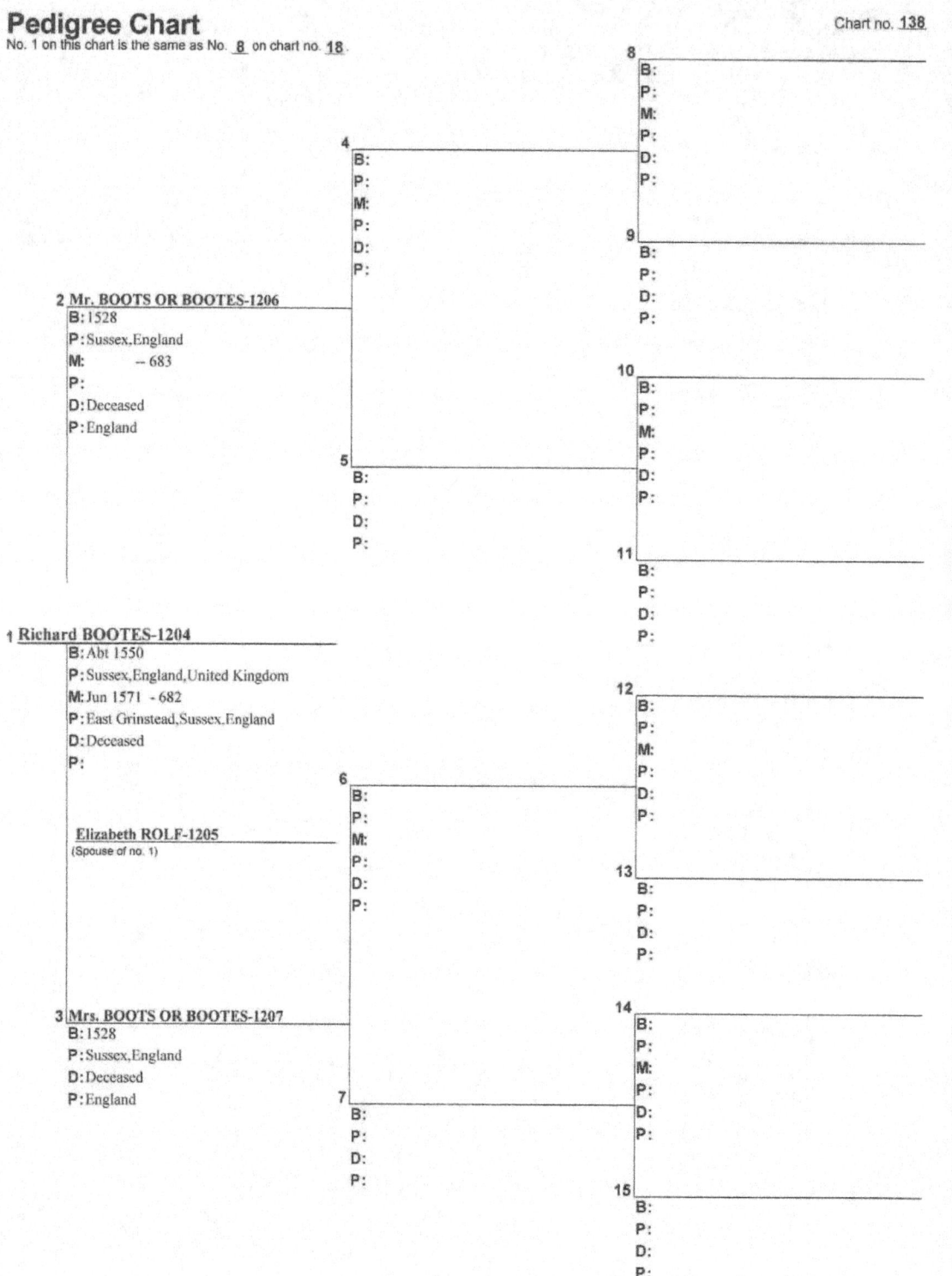

8
B:
P:
M:
P:
D:
P:

4
B:
P:
M:
P:
D:
P:

9
B:
P:
D:
P:

2 Mr. BOOTS OR BOOTES-1206
B: 1528
P: Sussex,England
M: -- 683
P:
D: Deceased
P: England

10
B:
P:
M:
P:
D:
P:

5
B:
P:
D:
P:

11
B:
P:
D:
P:

1 Richard BOOTES-1204
B: Abt 1550
P: Sussex,England,United Kingdom
M: Jun 1571 - 682
P: East Grinstead,Sussex,England
D: Deceased
P:

12
B:
P:
M:
P:
D:
P:

6
B:
P:
M:
P:
D:
P:

13
B:
P:
D:
P:

Elizabeth ROLF-1205
(Spouse of no. 1)

3 Mrs. BOOTS OR BOOTES-1207
B: 1528
P: Sussex,England
D: Deceased
P: England

14
B:
P:
M:
P:
D:
P:

7
B:
P:
D:
P:

15
B:
P:
D:
P:

06 Nov 2015

Pedigree Chart

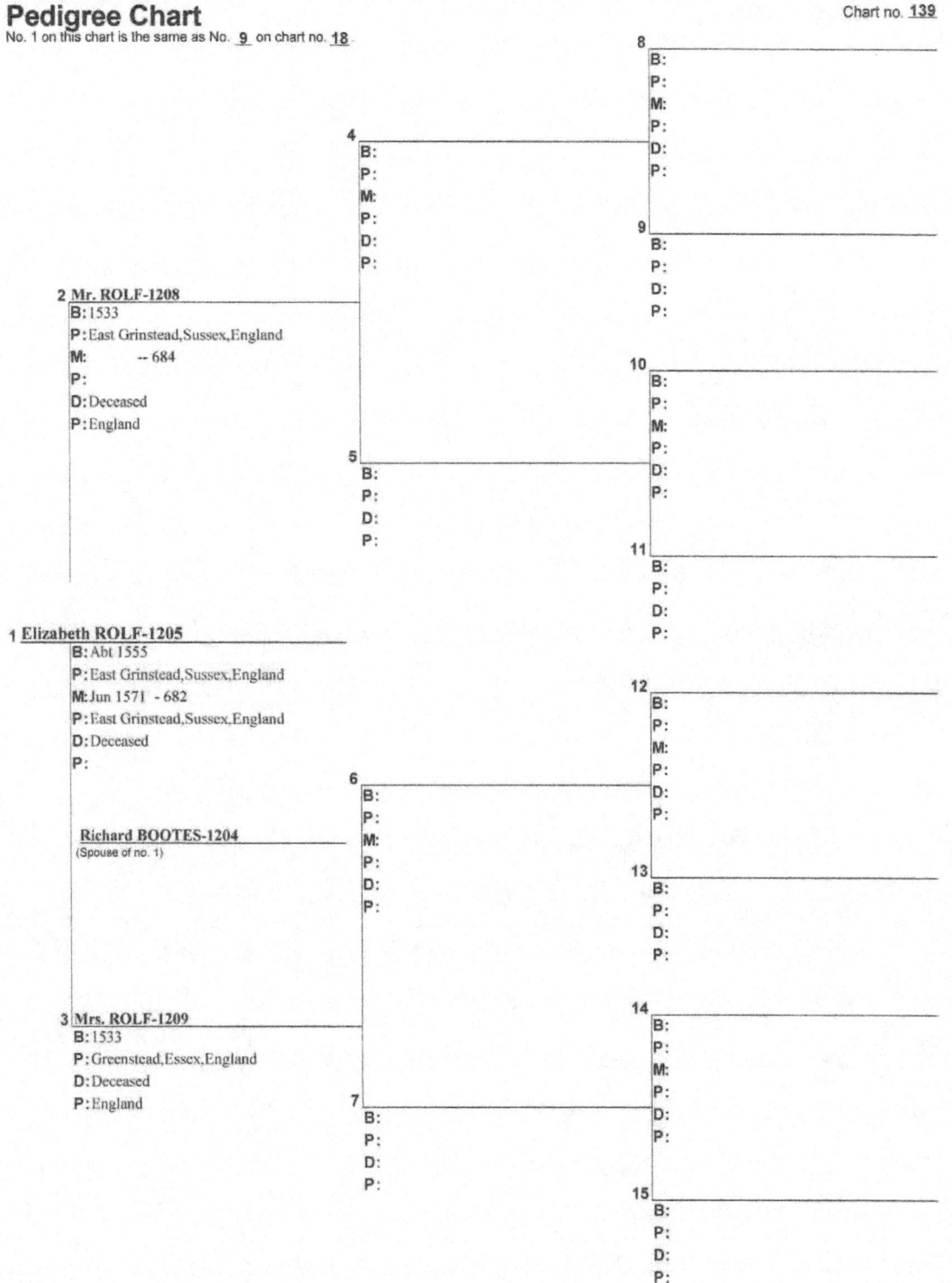

8
B:
P:
M:
P:
D:
P:

4
B:
P:
M:
P:
D:
P:

9
B:
P:
D:
P:

2 Mr. ROLF-1208
B: 1533
P: East Grinstead, Sussex, England
M: -- 684
P:
D: Deceased
P: England

10
B:
P:
M:
P:
D:
P:

5
B:
P:
D:
P:

11
B:
P:
D:
P:

1 Elizabeth ROLF-1205
B: Abt 1555
P: East Grinstead, Sussex, England
M: Jun 1571 - 682
P: East Grinstead, Sussex, England
D: Deceased
P:

12
B:
P:
M:
P:
D:
P:

Richard BOOTES-1204
(Spouse of no. 1)

6
B:
P:
M:
P:
D:
P:

13
B:
P:
D:
P:

3 Mrs. ROLF-1209
B: 1533
P: Greenstead, Essex, England
D: Deceased
P: England

14
B:
P:
M:
P:
D:
P:

7
B:
P:
D:
P:

15
B:
P:
D:
P:

06 Nov 2015

Pedigree Chart

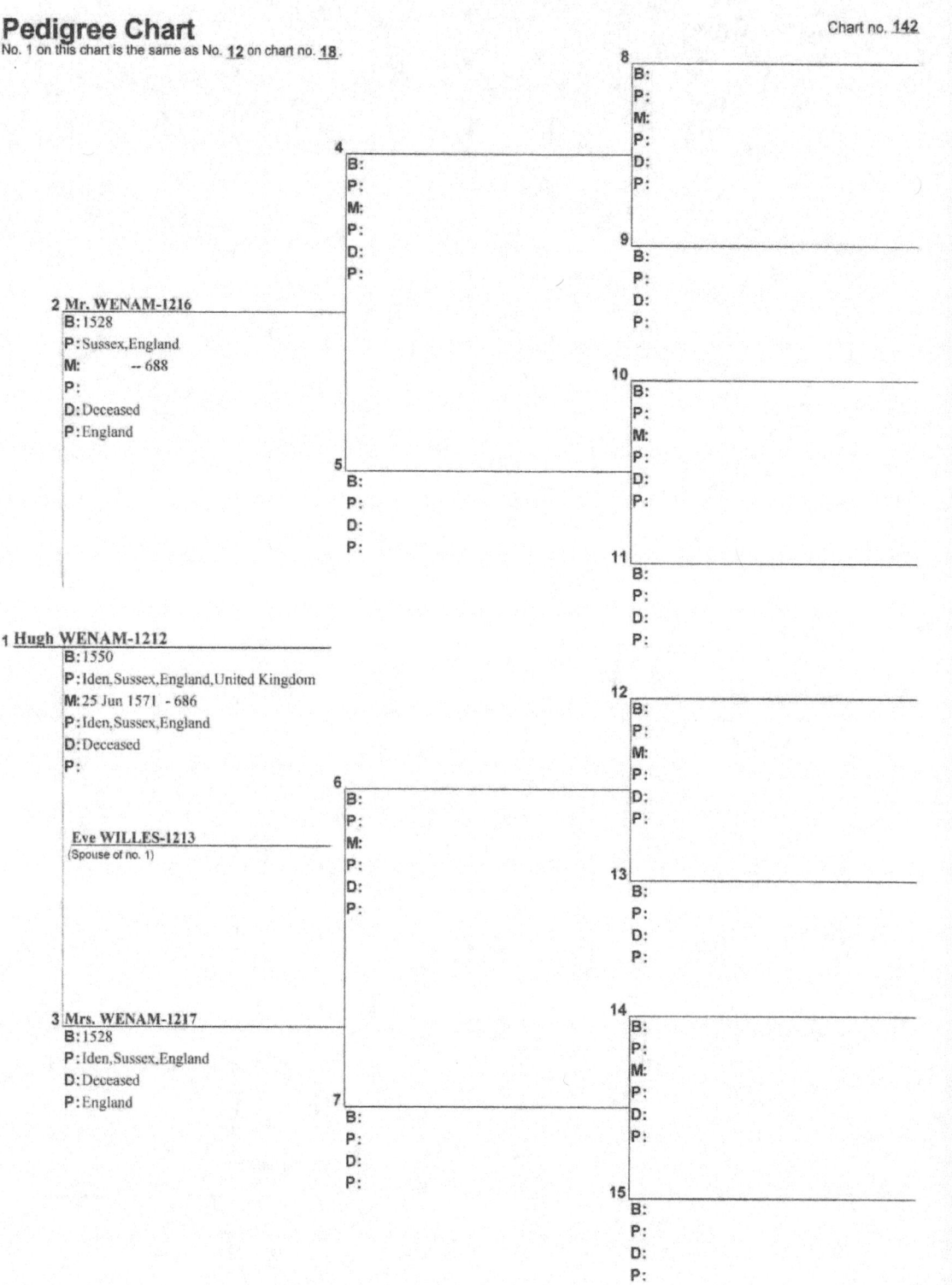

2 Mr. WENAM-1216
B: 1528
P: Sussex,England
M: -- 688
P:
D: Deceased
P: England

1 Hugh WENAM-1212
B: 1550
P: Iden,Sussex,England,United Kingdom
M: 25 Jun 1571 - 686
P: Iden,Sussex,England
D: Deceased
P:

Eve WILLES-1213
(Spouse of no. 1)

3 Mrs. WENAM-1217
B: 1528
P: Iden,Sussex,England
D: Deceased
P: England

4
B:
P:
M:
P:
D:
P:

5
B:
P:
D:
P:

6
B:
P:
M:
P:
D:
P:

7
B:
P:
D:
P:

8
B:
P:
M:
P:
D:
P:

9
B:
P:
D:
P:

10
B:
P:
M:
P:
D:
P:

11
B:
P:
D:
P:

12
B:
P:
M:
P:
D:
P:

13
B:
P:
D:
P:

14
B:
P:
M:
P:
D:
P:

15
B:
P:
D:
P:

06 Nov 2015

Pedigree Chart

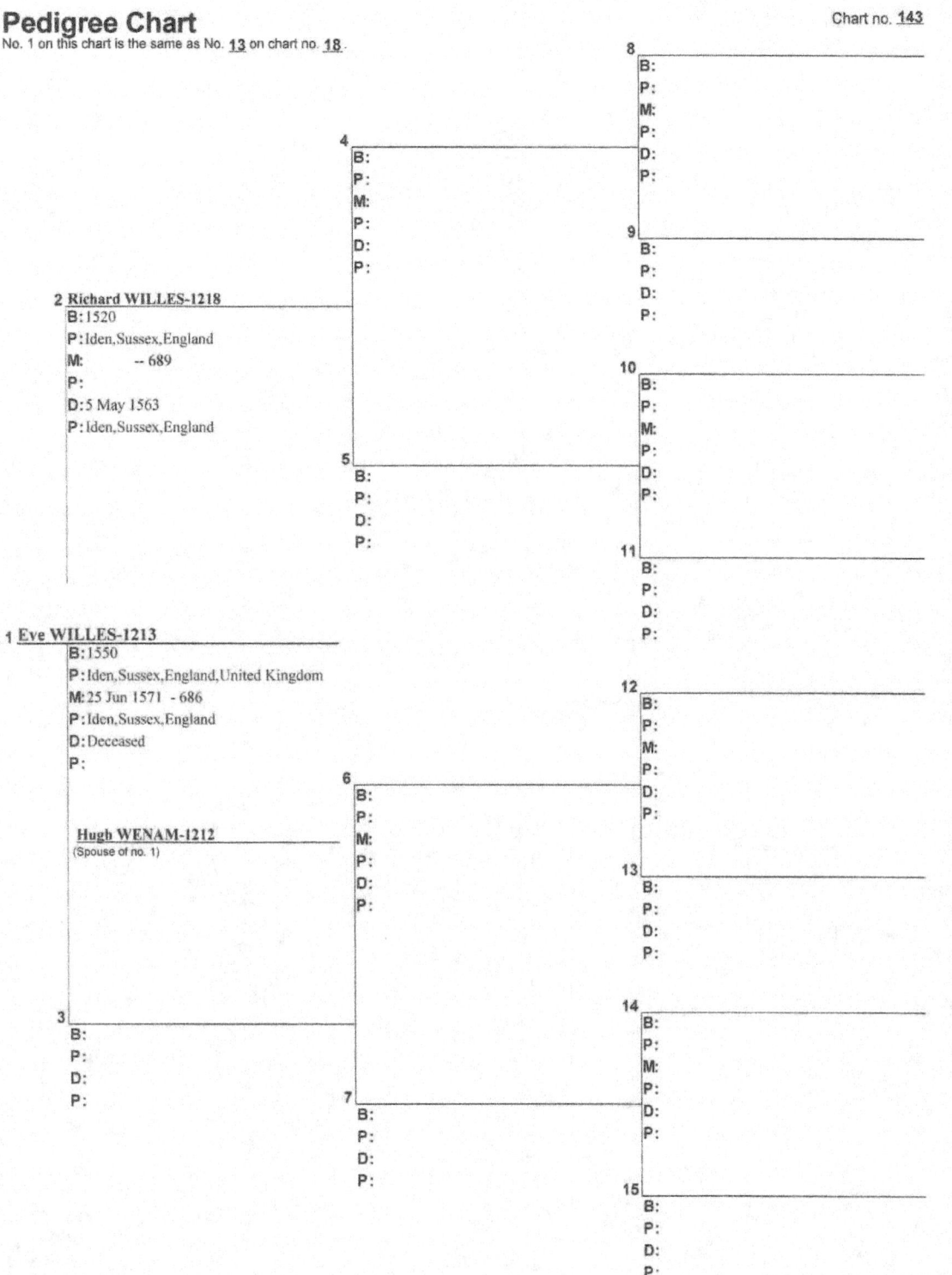

8
B:
P:
M:
P:
D:
P:

4
B:
P:
M:
P:
D:
P:

9
B:
P:
D:
P:

2 Richard WILLES-1218
B: 1520
P: Iden, Sussex, England
M: -- 689
P:
D: 5 May 1563
P: Iden, Sussex, England

10
B:
P:
M:
P:
D:
P:

5
B:
P:
D:
P:

11
B:
P:
D:
P:

1 Eve WILLES-1213
B: 1550
P: Iden, Sussex, England, United Kingdom
M: 25 Jun 1571 - 686
P: Iden, Sussex, England
D: Deceased
P:

12
B:
P:
M:
P:
D:
P:

Hugh WENAM-1212
(Spouse of no. 1)

6
B:
P:
M:
P:
D:
P:

13
B:
P:
D:
P:

3
B:
P:
D:
P:

14
B:
P:
M:
P:
D:
P:

7
B:
P:
D:
P:

15
B:
P:
D:
P:

06 Nov 2015

Pedigree Chart

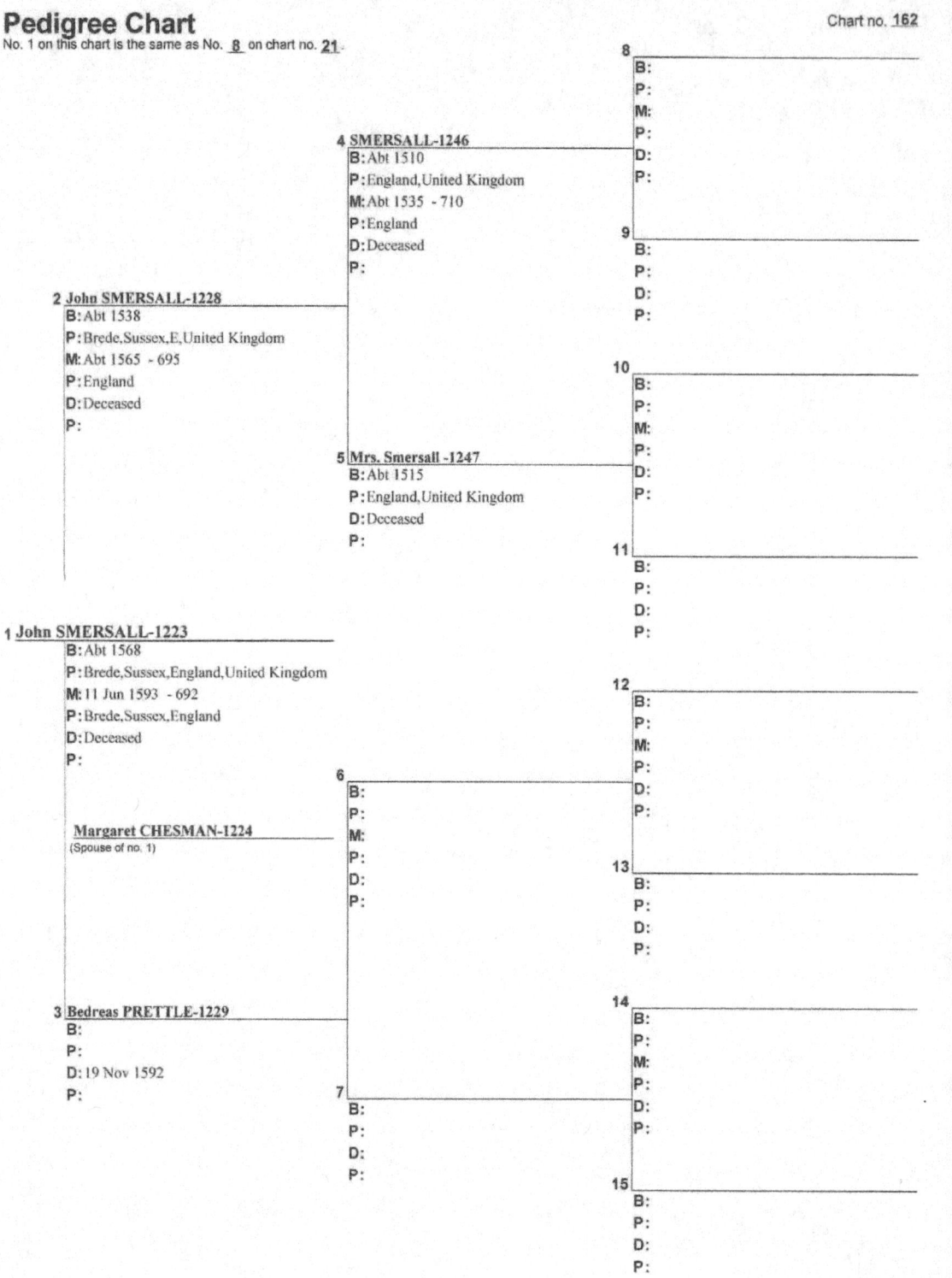

8
B:
P:
M:
P:
D:
P:

4 SMERSALL-1246
B: Abt 1510
P: England, United Kingdom
M: Abt 1535 - 710
P: England
D: Deceased
P:

9
B:
P:
D:
P:

2 John SMERSALL-1228
B: Abt 1538
P: Brede, Sussex, E, United Kingdom
M: Abt 1565 - 695
P: England
D: Deceased
P:

10
B:
P:
M:
P:
D:
P:

5 Mrs. Smersall -1247
B: Abt 1515
P: England, United Kingdom
D: Deceased
P:

11
B:
P:
D:
P:

1 John SMERSALL-1223
B: Abt 1568
P: Brede, Sussex, England, United Kingdom
M: 11 Jun 1593 - 692
P: Brede, Sussex, England
D: Deceased
P:

12
B:
P:
M:
P:
D:
P:

6
B:
P:
M:
P:
D:
P:

13
B:
P:
D:
P:

Margaret CHESMAN-1224
(Spouse of no. 1)

14
B:
P:
M:
P:
D:
P:

3 Bedreas PRETTLE-1229
B:
P:
D: 19 Nov 1592
P:

7
B:
P:
D:
P:

15
B:
P:
D:
P:

Pedigree Chart

No. 1 on this chart is the same as No. **9** on chart no. **21**.

Chart no. **163**

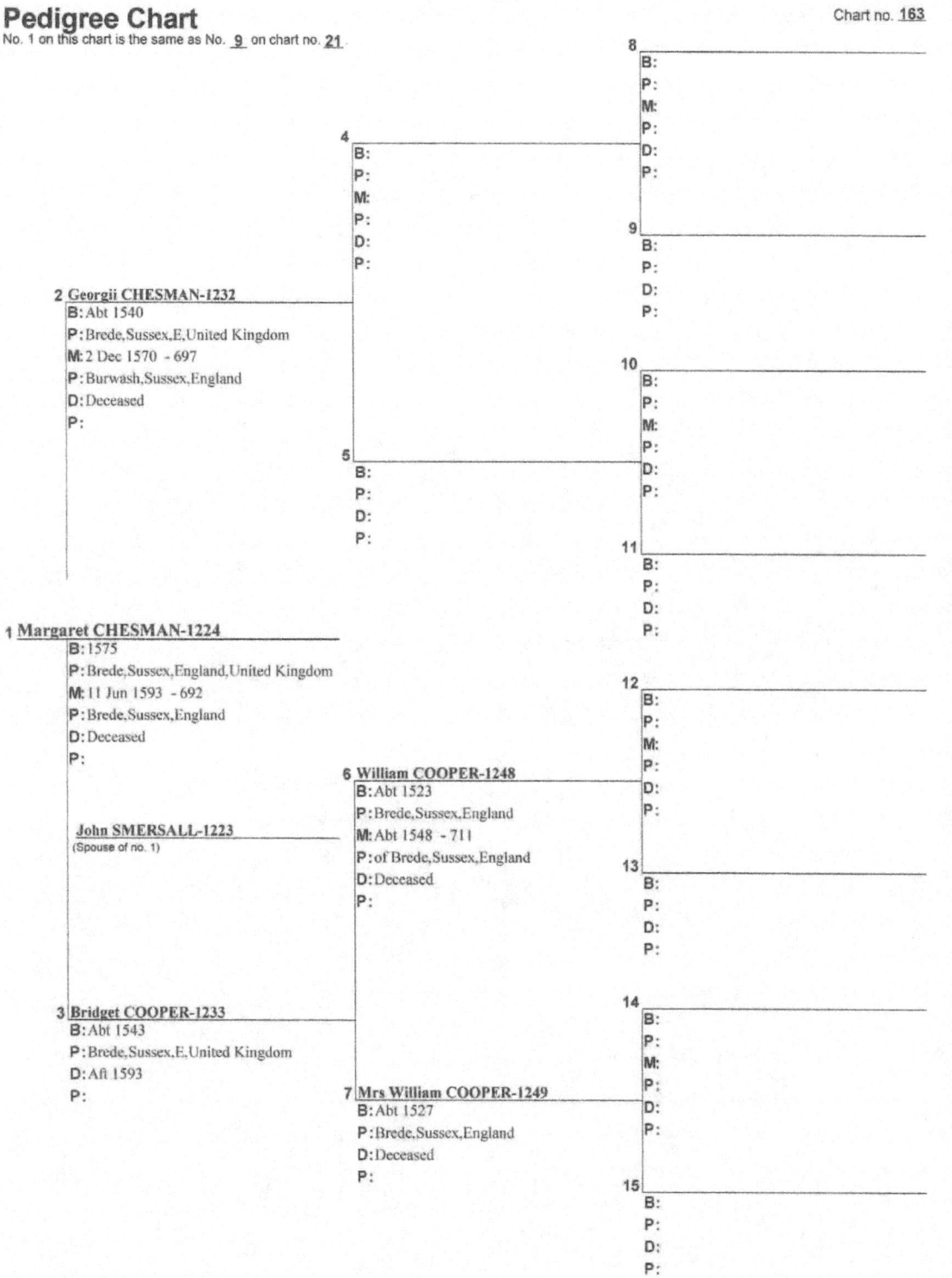

8
B:
P:
M:
P:
D:
P:

4
B:
P:
M:
P:
D:
P:

9
B:
P:
D:
P:

2 Georgii CHESMAN-1232
B: Abt 1540
P: Brede,Sussex,E,United Kingdom
M: 2 Dec 1570 - 697
P: Burwash,Sussex,England
D: Deceased
P:

10
B:
P:
M:
P:
D:
P:

5
B:
P:
D:
P:

11
B:
P:
D:
P:

1 Margaret CHESMAN-1224
B: 1575
P: Brede,Sussex,England,United Kingdom
M: 11 Jun 1593 - 692
P: Brede,Sussex,England
D: Deceased
P:

12
B:
P:
M:
P:
D:
P:

6 William COOPER-1248
B: Abt 1523
P: Brede,Sussex,England
M: Abt 1548 - 711
P: of Brede,Sussex,England
D: Deceased
P:

13
B:
P:
D:
P:

John SMERSALL-1223
(Spouse of no. 1)

14
B:
P:
M:
P:
D:
P:

3 Bridget COOPER-1233
B: Abt 1543
P: Brede,Sussex,E,United Kingdom
D: Aft 1593
P:

7 Mrs William COOPER-1249
B: Abt 1527
P: Brede,Sussex,England
D: Deceased
P:

15
B:
P:
D:
P:

08 Nov 2015

Pedigree Chart

No. 1 on this chart is the same as No. 10 on chart no. 21.

8 Walter BOURNE OR BORNE-1264
B: Abt 1474
P: Wick, Worcestershire, England
M: -- 724
P:
D: Aft 1532
P: Worcestershire, England

4 John BOURNE-1250
B: 1500
P: Bobbingworth, Essex, England
M: 1525 - 712
P: Bobbingworth,, Essex, England
D: 1561
P: Bobbingworth, Essex, England

9
B:
P:
D:
P:

2 William BOURNE-1234
B: Abt 1527
P: Bobbingworth, Essex, England
M: -- 698
P:
D: 29 Apr 1591
P: Bobbingworth, E, E, United Kingdom

10
B:
P:
M:
P:
D:
P:

5 Margaret -1251
B: 1505
P: Bobbingworth, Essex, England
D: 1564
P: England

11
B:
P:
D:
P:

1 Robert BOURNE-1225
B: Abt 1570
P: Bodiam, Sussex, E, United Kingdom
M: Abt 1593 - 693
P: Bodian,, Sussex, England
D: 28 Feb 1605
P: England, United Kingdom

12
B:
P:
M:
P:
D:
P:

6 Richard RYSE-1259
B: 1504
P: Bedford, B, England, United Kingdom
M: Abt 1529 - 720
P: Of, Bedford, England
D: Abt 1539
P: Bedfordshire, England

Susan MOORE-1226
(Spouse of no. 1)

13
B:
P:
D:
P:

3 Margaret RYSE-1235
B: 1531
P: Potter Newton, Yorkshire, England
D: 28 Dec 1594
P: Bobbingworth, E, E, United Kingdom

14
B:
P:
M:
P:
D:
P:

7 Mrs Richard RYSE-1260
B: 1507
P: Bedford, B, England, United Kingdom
D: 1536/1595
P:

15
B:
P:
D:
P:

Pedigree Chart

No. 1 on this chart is the same as No. __11__ on chart no. __21__ .

Chart no. __165__

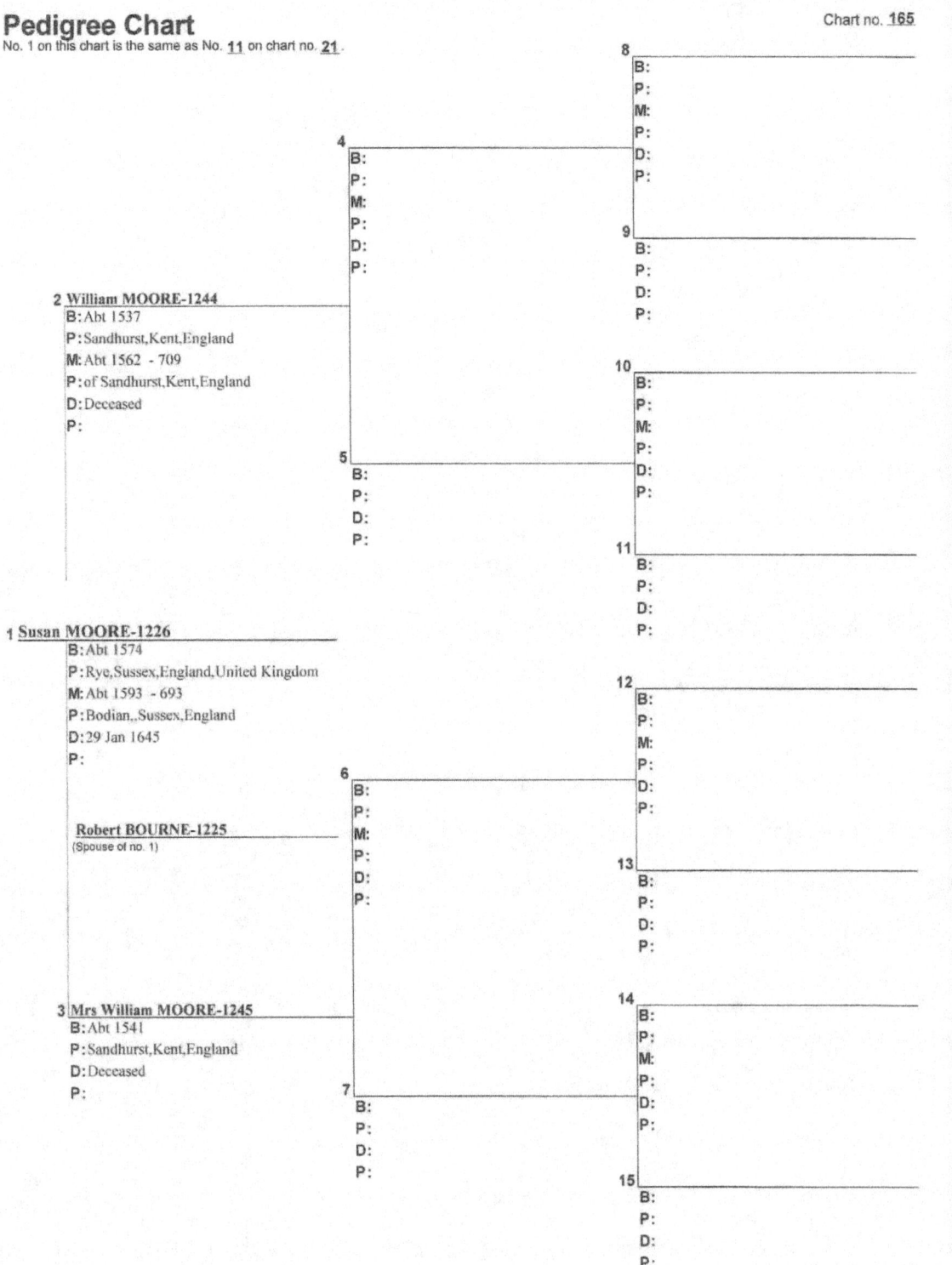

8
B:
P:
M:
P:
D:
P:

4
B:
P:
M:
P:
D:
P:

9
B:
P:
D:
P:

2 William MOORE-1244
B: Abt 1537
P: Sandhurst,Kent,England
M: Abt 1562 - 709
P: of Sandhurst,Kent,England
D: Deceased
P:

10
B:
P:
M:
P:
D:
P:

5
B:
P:
D:
P:

11
B:
P:
D:
P:

1 Susan MOORE-1226
B: Abt 1574
P: Rye,Sussex,England,United Kingdom
M: Abt 1593 - 693
P: Bodian,,Sussex,England
D: 29 Jan 1645
P:

12
B:
P:
M:
P:
D:
P:

6
B:
P:
M:
P:
D:
P:

Robert BOURNE-1225
(Spouse of no. 1)

13
B:
P:
D:
P:

3 Mrs William MOORE-1245
B: Abt 1541
P: Sandhurst,Kent,England
D: Deceased
P:

14
B:
P:
M:
P:
D:
P:

7
B:
P:
D:
P:

15
B:
P:
D:
P:

Pedigree Chart

No. 1 on this chart is the same as No. __8__ on chart no. __34__ .

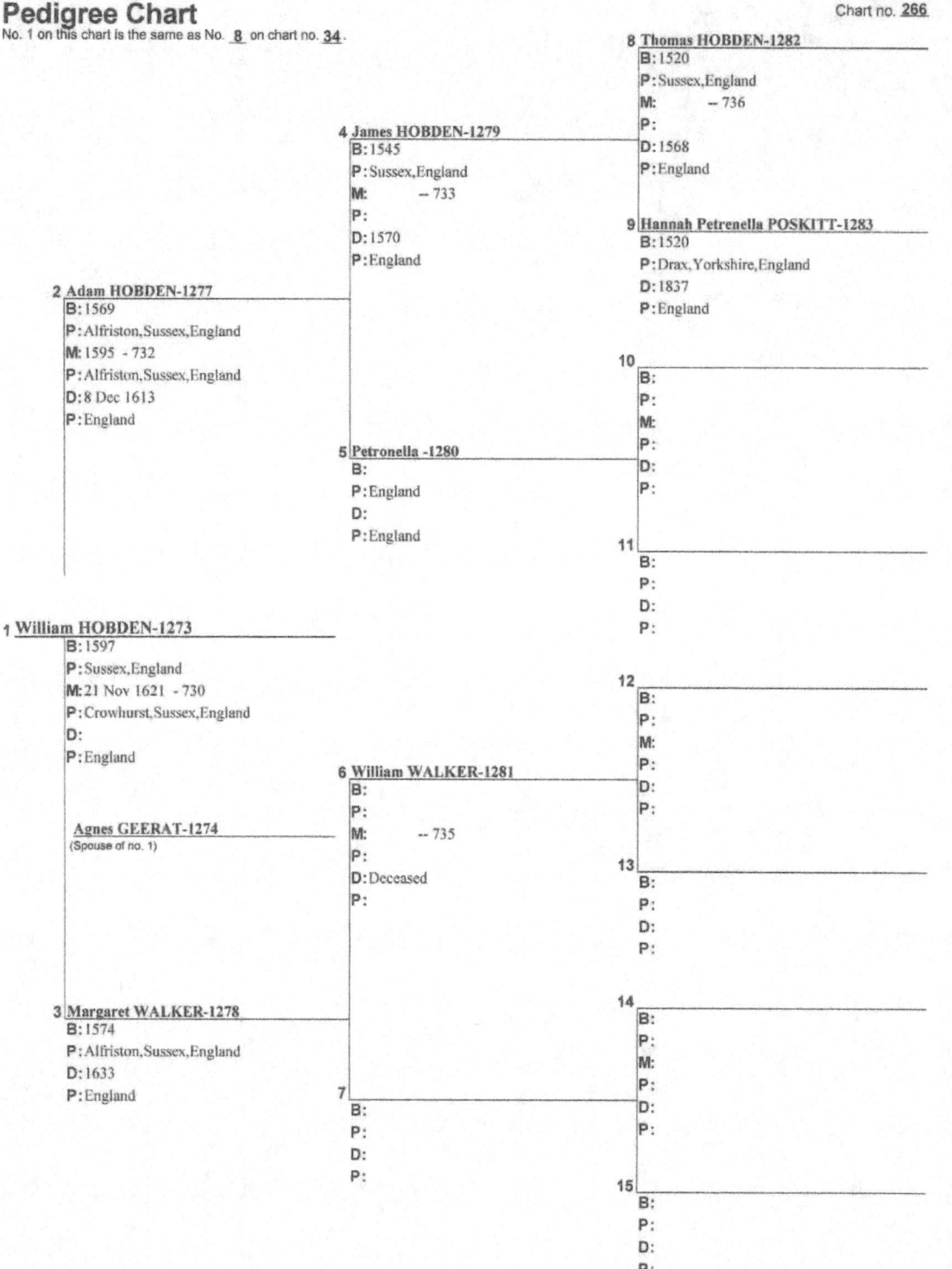

8 Thomas HOBDEN-1282
B: 1520
P: Sussex, England
M: – 736
P:
D: 1568
P: England

4 James HOBDEN-1279
B: 1545
P: Sussex, England
M: – 733
P:
D: 1570
P: England

9 Hannah Petrenella POSKITT-1283
B: 1520
P: Drax, Yorkshire, England
D: 1837
P: England

2 Adam HOBDEN-1277
B: 1569
P: Alfriston, Sussex, England
M: 1595 – 732
P: Alfriston, Sussex, England
D: 8 Dec 1613
P: England

10
B:
P:
M:
P:
D:
P:

5 Petronella -1280
B:
P: England
D:
P: England

11
B:
P:
D:
P:

1 William HOBDEN-1273
B: 1597
P: Sussex, England
M: 21 Nov 1621 – 730
P: Crowhurst, Sussex, England
D:
P: England

12
B:
P:
M:
P:
D:
P:

6 William WALKER-1281
B:
P:
M: -- 735
P:
D: Deceased
P:

Agnes GEERAT-1274
(Spouse of no. 1)

13
B:
P:
D:
P:

14
B:
P:
M:
P:
D:
P:

3 Margaret WALKER-1278
B: 1574
P: Alfriston, Sussex, England
D: 1633
P: England

7
B:
P:
D:
P:

15
B:
P:
D:
P:

06 Nov 2015

Pedigree Chart
Alphabetical Index

RIN	Name	Born /BR	Died /Bur	Found on Chart	Position
1298	, _____ Laurs...	Abt 1636	Deceased	72	4
1269	, Anne		Deceased	27	7
1267	, Baker	Abt 1603	Deceased	21	7
1154	, Blackwell	Abt 1575	Deceased	11	9
578	, Christians	1705	Deceased	6	14
1220	, Collins	Abt 1615	Deceased	20	5
1203	, Elinor	Abt 1582	Deceased	18	5
564	, Elizabeth	Abt 1693	Deceased	2	13
576	, Hans	1710	Deceased	6	10
582	, Hans	1685	Deceased	7	10
1199	, Hues	Abt 1590	Deceased	11	15
575	, Jens	1710	Deceased	6	8
558	, Joblin	Abt 1685	Deceased	2	11
585	, Johanne	1710	Deceased	7	13
584	, Jorgens	1710	Deceased	7	12
1167	, Juliana	Abt 1520	Oct 1563	84	7
581	, Karen	1680	Deceased	7	9
577	, Lars	1695	Deceased	6	12
1299	, Laurs	Abt 1640	Deceased	72	5
586	, Mads	1710	Deceased	7	14
583	, Maren	1685	Deceased	7	11
1023	, Margaret	Abt 1649	Deceased	20	3
1251	, Margaret	1505	1564	164	5
1160	, Marie	Abt 1548	Deceased	85	3
295	, Mary		Deceased	4	7
579	, Nelie	1705	Deceased	6	15
580	, Niels	1680	Deceased	7	8
1296	, Peder	Abt 1630	Deceased	66	4
1280	, Petronella			266	5
1041	, Rasmus	Abt 1674	Deceased	73	2
1042	, Rasmus	Abt 1676	Deceased	73	3
1247	, Smersall	Abt 1515	Deceased	162	5
566	, Susanna	Abt 1647	Deceased	3	9
587	, Susanne	1710	Deceased	7	15
135	ALLEN, Elizabeth	1740	5 Sep 1782	3	3
590	ANDERSEN, Hans	Abt 1695	Deceased	9	10
1033	ANDERSEN, Poufvel	17 Jan 1664	Deceased	69	2
556	BACKWELL, Ann	7 May 1676	Deceased	2	9
1266	BAKER,	Abt 1600	Deceased	21	6
1025	BAKER, Ann	Abt 1633	Deceased	21	3
569	BALLARD, John	1683	4 Aug 1752	4	8
136	BALLARD, John	16 Oct 1757	24 May 1845	4	2
67	BALLARD, John	20 Feb 1784	1855	1	10
292	BALLARD, John	2 Mar 1714	14 Nov 1776	4	4
33	BALLARD, Lydia Mary	24 Oct 1814	12 Feb 1885	1	5
301	BERWICK, Ann	Abt 1728	1806	5	5
573	BERWICK, Thomas	1700	Jul 1770	5	10
1015	BLACKWELL, Henry	16 Sep 1632	Deceased	11	2
1153	BLACKWELL, Humfrey	Abt 1570	Deceased	11	8
1151	BLACKWELL, Humfrey	Abt 1600	Deceased	11	4
289	BLUNDELL, Mary	Abt 1722	Deceased	2	7
1222	BOORNE OR BOURNE, Dorothy	Abt 1608	Deceased	21	5
565	BOOTES, James	13 Jun 1645	13 May 1705	3	8
1020	BOOTES, James	10 May 1608	24 Oct 1667	18	2
290	BOOTES, James	21 May 1699	13 Aug 1741	3	4
1202	BOOTES, Richard	Abt 1578	30 May 1633	18	4
1204	BOOTES, Richard	Abt 1550	Deceased	18	8
134	BOOTS, Bartholomew	25 Apr 1736	16 Sep 1806	3	2
66	BOOTS, Frances	29 Dec 1771	2 Nov 1852	1	9
1207	BOOTS OR BOOTES,	1528	Deceased	138	3
1206	BOOTS OR BOOTES,	1528	Deceased	138	2
1250	BOURNE, John	1500	1561	164	4
1264	BOURNE OR BORNE, Walter	Abt 1474	Aft 1532	164	8
1225	BOURNE, Robert	Abt 1570	28 Feb 1605	21	10
1234	BOURNE, William	Abt 1527	29 Apr 1591	164	2
1293	BRIGHTRIDGE, John	Abt 1648	Deceased	34	6

Pedigree Chart
Alphabetical Index

RIN	Name	Born /BR	Died /Bur	Found on Chart	Position
1029	BRIGHTRIDGE, Mary	Abt 1668	3 Jun 1712	34	3
1141	BROOKER, Grace	1584	Deceased	10	5
1294	CARMAN, Ellinor	Abt 1652	Deceased	34	7
1232	CHESMAN, Georgii	Abt 1540	Deceased	163	2
1224	CHESMAN, Margaret	1575	Deceased	21	9
142	CHRISTENSEN, Hans	Abt 1754	20 Aug 1814	7	2
1035	CHRISTENSEN, Jens	<1695>	Deceased	71	2
306	CHRISTIANSDATTER, Birthe	Abt 1731		6	7
140	CHRISTOPHERSEN, Mads	Abt 1761	14 Jun 1845	6	2
1219	COLLINS,	Abt 1610	Deceased	20	4
291	COLLINS, Anne	4 Nov 1693	Aft 1736	3	5
1022	COLLINS, Thomas	Abt 1644	Deceased	20	2
567	COLLINS, William	5 Jun 1672	Deceased	3	10
1152	COMBER, Agnis	Abt 1600	Deceased	11	5
1155	COMBER, John	Abt 1572	Oct 1625	11	10
1157	COMBER, Leonard	Abt 1534	Feb 1579	84	2
1163	COMBER, William	Abt 1503	Deceased	84	4
1164	COMBER, William	Abt 1507	Deceased	84	5
1233	COOPER, Bridget	Abt 1543	Aft 1593	163	3
1249	COOPER, Mrs William	Abt 1527	Deceased	163	7
1248	COOPER, William	Abt 1523	Deceased	163	6
1147	DEPRON, Elizabeth	1572	Deceased	10	9
1295	DURRANT, Ambrose		Deceased	37	6
1031	DURRANT, Elizabeth	1684		37	3
1158	FARNCOMBE, Margaret	Abt 1540	Deceased	84	3
1166	FARNCOMBE, Richard	Abt 1514	Jul 1564	84	6
1013	FREEMAN, Elizabeth	1632	1701	10	3
1274	GEERAT, Agnes			34	9
1030	GLAZIER, John	1682		37	2
574	GLAZIER, Lucy	1704	Sep 1767	5	11
288	GLOVER, John	Abt 1723	23 Nov 1748	2	6
563	GLOVER, Robert	Abt 1689	Deceased	2	12
133	GLOVER, Sarah Blundell	Abt 1743	1812	2	3
1150	GOODSALL,	1550	Deceased	74	2
284	GOODSALL, John	8 Mar 1710	Deceased	2	4
1146	GOODSALL, John	1572	Deceased	10	8
132	GOODSALL, Thomas	1734	1813	2	2
16	GOODSELL, Alfred	5 Jan 1851	29 Jul 1898	1	2
32	GOODSELL, John	24 Jul 1793	12 Sep 1855	1	4
65	GOODSELL, John	19 Jul 1767	4 Oct 1840	1	8
8	GOODSELL, Joseph Franklin	21 Feb 1886	21 Sep 1934	1	1
1140	GUDSALL, Thomas	1591	1629	10	4
1156	GUNN, Leatyce	2 Apr 1570	Deceased	11	11
1159	GUNN, Richard	Abt 1548	Deceased	85	2
555	GUTSALL, James	16 Feb 1672	Deceased	2	8
1012	GUTSELL, Thomas	13 Sep 1621	27 Feb 1680	10	2
293	HALLADAY, Elizabeth	1731	15 Apr 1764	4	5
303	HANSDATTER, Kirsten	1735	Deceased	6	5
145	HANSDATTER, Maren	1769	Bef 1834	8	3
70	HANSDATTER, Pernille	4 Mar 1789	13 Jun 1867	1	13
1034	HANSEN, Anne		Deceased	69	3
72	HANSEN, Anne Catrine	27 Jun 1801	14 Jan 1841	1	15
309	HANSEN, Kirsten	Abt 1709	Deceased	7	5
312	HANSEN, Lars	Abt 1731	Deceased	8	4
314	HANSEN, Mette Sophie	Abt 1720	13 Sep 1793	9	5
1277	HOBDEN, Adam	1569	8 Dec 1613	266	2
300	HOBDEN, Edward	27 Aug 1732	24 Dec 1808	5	4
1279	HOBDEN, James	1545	1570	266	4
68	HOBDEN, Mary	2 Feb 1790	15 Mar 1833	1	11
138	HOBDEN, Richard	Abt 1756	Deceased	5	2
571	HOBDEN, Thomas	1700	16 Jan 1768	5	8
1271	HOBDEN, Thomas	Abt 1634	Deceased	34	4
1282	HOBDEN, Thomas	1520	1568	266	8
1273	HOBDEN, William	1597		34	8
1028	HOBDEN, William	4 Mar 1664	25 May 1734	34	2
9	HOOPES, Olive Emeline	29 Jul 1881	3 Jun 1962	1	Spouse

Pedigree Chart
Alphabetical Index

RIN	Name	Born /BR	Died /Bur	Found on Chart	Position
1198	HUES,	Abt 1585	Deceased	11	14
1194	HUES, Judith	Abt 1613	Deceased	11	7
572	HUMPHREY, Catherine	1700	Deceased	5	9
302	JENSEN, Christopher	1735	Deceased	6	4
17	JENSEN, Hannah Christina	24 Aug 1853	17 Jun 1888	1	3
34	JENSEN, Hans	6 Aug 1825		1	6
593	JENSEN, Mette	7 Apr 1713	11 Mar 1761	9	13
285	JOBLIN, Ann	1712	1758	2	5
557	JOBLING,		Deceased	2	10
310	JORGENSEN, Lars	Abt 1733	Deceased	7	6
1016	LAKER, Judith	11 Mar 1637	Deceased	11	3
1196	LAKER, Mary	1585	Deceased	11	13
1193	LAKER, Thomas	Abt 1609	Deceased	11	6
1195	LAKER, William	1585	Deceased	11	12
35	LARSDATTER, Maren	29 Jul 1830	9 Feb 1906	1	7
143	LARSDATTER, Susanne	Abt 1748	20 Feb 1819	7	3
144	LARSEN, Niels	5 Jun 1757	14 Mar 1846	8	2
305	LARSEN, Niels	1717	Deceased	6	6
315	LAURITZSEN, Mads	Abt 1736	19 Aug 1818	9	6
1040	LAURSEN, Peder	Abt 1665	Deceased	72	3
1039	LAURSEN, Peder	Abt 1661	Apr 1736	72	2
316	MADSDATTER, Anne Catrine	1737	7 Jun 1790	9	7
311	MADSDATTER, Pernille	Abt 1737	Deceased	7	7
69	MADSEN, Jens	Abt 1799	27 Apr 1841	1	12
147	MADSEN, Kirsten	20 Nov 1768	19 Oct 1837	9	3
592	MADSEN, Lauritz	1705	Deceased	9	12
1245	MOORE, Mrs William	Abt 1541	Deceased	165	3
1226	MOORE, Susan	Abt 1574	29 Jan 1645	21	11
1244	MOORE, William	Abt 1537	Deceased	165	2
1027	MORRIS, Jane	8 Feb 1637	28 Feb 1716	27	3
1268	MORRIS, John	Abt 1615	Deceased	27	6
1270	MORRIS, John	Abt 1590	Deceased	27	12
1036	NIELSDATTER, Annie	<1699>	Deceased	71	3
141	NIELSDATTER, Bertha	Abt 1771	1814	6	3
308	NIELSEN, Christen	Abt 1705	Deceased	7	4
71	NIELSEN, Lars	14 Jan 1793	17 May 1872	1	14
1272	PARKER, Jane	1639	1728	34	5
1275	PARKER, John	3 May 1617	Deceased	34	10
594	PEDERSEN, Mads	1693	23 Nov 1755	9	14
313	PEDERSEN, Soren	10 May 1722	25 May 1798	9	4
1032	PEDERSEN, Terchel	Abt 1644	1713	66	2
1283	POSKITT, Hannah Petrenella	1520	1837	266	9
1297	POUFVELSEN, Anders		Deceased	69	4
591	POVELSEN, Maren	Abt 1694	19 Jun 1753	9	11
1229	PRETTLE, Bedreas		19 Nov 1592	162	3
595	RASMUSDATTER, Anne Cathrine	1700	28 Nov 1762	9	15
589	RASMUSDATTER, Bodil	1680	Deceased	9	9
137	RELFE, Ann	1760	11 Feb 1825	4	3
294	RELFE, Thomas		Deceased	4	6
1208	ROLF,	1533	Deceased	139	2
1209	ROLF,	1533	Deceased	139	3
1205	ROLF, Elizabeth	Abt 1555	Deceased	18	9
1235	RYSE, Margaret	1531	28 Dec 1594	164	3
1260	RYSE, Mrs Richard	1507	1536/1595	164	7
1259	RYSE, Richard	1504	Abt 1539	164	6
1214	SAINTGEORGE,	1548	Deceased	18	14
1215	SAINTGEORGE,	1548	Deceased	18	15
1211	SAINTGEORGE, Anne	1570	Deceased	18	7
1246	SMERSALL,	Abt 1510	Deceased	162	4
1221	SMERSALL, John the Third	Abt 1604	Deceased	21	4
1223	SMERSALL, John	Abt 1568	Deceased	21	8
1228	SMERSALL, John	Abt 1538	Deceased	162	2
568	SMERSWELL, Susanna	1661	Deceased	3	11
1024	SMERSWELL, William	Abt 1630	Deceased	21	2
146	SORENSEN, Hans	17 Jun 1759	26 Mar 1849	9	2
1026	STEPHENS, Ferdinando	1628	1 Jun 1703	27	2

Pedigree Chart

Alphabetical Index

RIN	Name	Born /BR	Died /Bur	Found on Chart	Position
570	STEVENS, Margaret	1684	Deceased	4	9
588	TERCHELSEN, Peder	1675	1740	9	8
1276	TREE, Judith	1617		34	11
139	VINCENT, Elizabeth	Abt 1760	5 May 1830	5	3
1278	WALKER, Margaret	1574	1633	266	3
1281	WALKER, William		Deceased	266	6
1217	WENAM,	1528	Deceased	142	3
1216	WENAM,	1528	Deceased	142	2
1212	WENAM, Hugh	1550	Deceased	18	12
1021	WENHAM, Anne	2 Oct 1608	1681	18	3
1210	WENHAM, William	23 Oct 1569	Deceased	18	6
1213	WILLES, Eve	1550	Deceased	18	13
1218	WILLES, Richard	1520	5 May 1563	143	2

Ahnentafel Chart for Joseph Franklin GOODSELL-8

First Generation

1. **Joseph Franklin GOODSELL**-8 was born on 21 Feb 1886 in Newton, Cache, Utah Territory, United States. He died on 21 Sep 1934 in Port Angeles, Clallam, Washington, United States. He was buried on 26 Sep 1934 in Weston, Franklin, Idaho, United States.

   Joseph married (MRIN:4) **Olive Emeline HOOPES**-9, daughter of Daniel Lewis HOOPES-18 and Catherine Heaver CLARKE-19 (MRIN:9), on 4 Oct 1905 in Logan City, Cache, Utah. Olive was born on 29 Jul 1881 in Weston, Oneida, Idaho Territory, United States. She died on 3 Jun 1962 in El Monte, Los Angeles, California, United States. She was buried on 14 Jun 1962 in Weston, Franklin, Idaho, United States.

Second Generation

2. **Alfred GOODSELL**-16 was born on 5 Jan 1851 in Hastings, Sussex, England. He was christened in 1856 in All Saints, Hastings, Sussex, England. He died on 29 Jul 1898 in Newton, Cache, Utah, United States. He was buried on 1 Aug 1898 in Newton, Cache, Utah, United States. Alfred married (MRIN:8) Hannah Christina JENSEN-17 on 25 Jul 1870 in Newton, Cache, Utah Territory, United States.

3. **Hannah Christina JENSEN**-17 was born on 24 Aug 1853 in Mønge, Vejby, Frederiksborg, Denmark. She was christened on 2 Oct 1853 in Vejby, Holbo, Frederiksborg, Denmark. She died on 17 Jun 1888 in Newton, Cache, Utah Territory, United States. She was buried on 20 Jun 1888 in Newton Cemetery, Cache, Utah, United States.

Third Generation

4. **John GOODSELL**-32 was born on 24 Jul 1793 in Hastings, Sussex, England. He was christened on 14 Aug 1793 in Hastings, Sussex, England, United Kingdom. He died on 12 Sep 1855 in St.Mary Magdalen, St. Leonard-On-Sea, Sussex, England. He was buried on 12 Sep 1855 in Hastings, Sussex, England, United Kingdom. John married (MRIN:16) Lydia Mary BALLARD-33 on 28 Dec 1833 in Hastings, Sussex, England, United Kingdom.

5. **Lydia Mary BALLARD**-33 was born on 24 Oct 1814 in Ashburnham, Sussex, England. She was christened on 19 Nov 1815 in Herstmonceux, Sussex, England. She died on 12 Feb 1885 in Newton, Cache, Utah Territory, United States. She was buried on 12 Feb 1885 in Newton, Cache, Utah Territory, United States.

6. **Hans JENSEN**-34 was born on 6 Aug 1825 in Vejby, Holbo, Frederiksborg, Denmark. He was christened on 7 Aug 1825 in Vejby, Holbo, Frederiksborg, Denmark. He died in Vejby, Vejby, Holbo, Frederiksborg, Denmark. Hans married (MRIN:17) Maren LARSDATTER-35 on 2 May 1853 in Hillerød, Frederiksborg, Denmark.

7. **Maren LARSDATTER**-35 was born on 29 Jul 1830 in Mønge, Vejby, Holbo, Frederiksborg, Denmark. She died on 9 Feb 1906 in Newton, Cache, Utah, United States. She was buried in Feb 1906 in Weston, Franklin, Idaho, United States.

Fourth Generation

8. **John GOODSELL**-65 was christened on 19 Jul 1767 in Salehurst, Sussex, England. He died on 4 Oct 1840 in Hastings, Sussex, England. He was buried on 9 Oct 1840 in Hastings, Sussex, England. John married (MRIN:33) Frances BOOTS-66 on 16 Oct 1791 in Hastings, Sussex, England.

9. **Frances BOOTS**-66 was born in Robertsbridge, Sussex, England. She was christened on 29 Dec 1771 in Salehurst, Sussex, England. She died on 2 Nov 1852 in St. Mary In The Castle, Hastings, Sussex, England. She was buried on 5 Nov 1852 in Hastings, Sussex, England.

10. **John BALLARD**-67 was born on 20 Feb 1784 in Burwash, Sussex, England. He was christened on 21 Mar 1784 in Burwash, Sussex, England. He died in 1855 in Ashburnham, Sussex, England. John married (MRIN:34) Mary HOBDEN-68 on 1 May 1809 in Dallington, Sussex, England.

11. **Mary HOBDEN**-68 was born on 2 Feb 1790 in Battle, Sussex, England. She was christened on 1 May 1790 in Battle, Sussex, England. She died on 15 Mar 1833 in Ashburnham, Sussex, England.

12. **Jens MADSEN**-69 was born about 1799 in Vejby, Frederiksborg, Denmark. He died on 27 Apr 1841 in Vejby, Frederiksborg, Denmark. He was buried on 27 Apr 1841 in Vejby, Frederiksborg, Denmark. Jens married (MRIN:35) Pernille HANSDATTER-70 about 1824 in , , Den.

13. **Pernille HANSDATTER**-70 was born on 4 Mar 1789 in Tågerup, Ramløse, Frederiksborg, Denmark. She was christened on 4 Mar 1789 in Tågerup, Ramløse, Frederiksborg, Denmark. She died on 13 Jun 1867 in Vejby, Frederiksborg, Denmark. She was buried on 8 Jan 1797.

14. **Lars NIELSEN**-71 was born on 14 Jan 1793 in Husby, Husby, Odense, Denmark. He was christened on 14 Jan 1793 in Husby, Odense, Denmark. He died on 17 May 1872 in Kindstrup, Gelsted, Vends, Odense, Denmark. He was buried on 24 May 1872 in Gelsted, Odense, Denmark. Lars married (MRIN:36) Anne Catrine HANSEN-72 on 26 Feb 1825 in Husby, Husby, Odense, Denmark.

15. **Anne Catrine HANSEN**-72 was born on 27 Jun 1801 in Kindstrup, Gelsted, Odense, Denmark. She was christened on 27 Jun 1801 in Gelsted, Odense, Denmark. She died on 14 Jan 1841 in Gelsted, Odense, Denmark. She was buried on 23 Jan 1841 in Gelsted, Odense, Denmark.

Fifth Generation

16. **Thomas GOODSALL**-132 was born in 1734 in Ewhurst, Sussex, England. He was christened on 7 Jul 1734 in Salehurst, Sussex, England. He died in 1813. He was buried on 4 Dec 1813. Thomas married (MRIN:67) Sarah Blundell GLOVER-133 on 22 Apr 1764 in Ewhurst, Sussex, England.

17. **Sarah Blundell GLOVER**-133 was born about 1743 in Salehurst, Sussex, England, United Kingdom. She was christened on 6 Nov 1743 in Bodiam, Sussex, England, United Kingdom. She died in 1812. She was buried on 27 Jan 1812 in Salehurst, Sussex, England, United Kingdom.

18. **Bartholomew BOOTS**-134 was born on 25 Apr 1736 in Bodiam, Sussex, England. He was christened on 25 Apr 1736 in Bodiam, Sussex, England. He died on 16 Sep 1806 in Northiam, Sussex, England. He was buried on 16 Sep 1806 in Northiam, Sussex, England. Bartholomew married (MRIN:68) Elizabeth ALLEN-135 on 17 May 1767 in Salehurst, Sussex, England.

19. **Elizabeth ALLEN**-135 was born in 1740 in Salehurst, Sussex, England, United Kingdom. She was christened on 13 May 1767 in Salehurst, Sussex, England. She died on 5 Sep 1782 in Salehurst, Sussex, England. She was buried on 5 Sep 1782 in Salehurst, Sussex, England, United Kingdom.

20. **John BALLARD**-136 was born on 16 Oct 1757 in Catsfield, Sussex, England. He was christened on

16 Oct 1757 in Catsfield, Sussex, England. He died on 24 May 1845 in Brighton, Sussex, England. John married (MRIN:69) Ann RELFE-137 on 15 Oct 1781 in Burwash, Sussex, England.

21. **Ann RELFE**-137 was born in 1760 in England. She was christened on 26 Oct 1761 in Biddenden, Kent, England. She died on 11 Feb 1825 in England.

22. **Richard HOBDEN**-138 was born about 1756 in Penhurst, Sussex, England, United Kingdom. He died. Richard married (MRIN:70) Elizabeth VINCENT-139 on 1 May 1782 in Penhurst, Sussex, England.

23. **Elizabeth VINCENT**-139 was born about 1760 in Penhurst, Sussex, England. She died on 5 May 1830 in Penhurst, Sussex, England.

24. **Mads CHRISTOPHERSEN**-140 was born about 1761 in Vejby, Frederiksborg, Denmark. He died on 14 Jun 1845 in Vejby, Frederiksborg, Denmark. He was buried on 21 Sep 1760 in Tørring, Ringkøbing, Denmark. Mads married (MRIN:71) Bertha NIELSDATTER-141 about 1792 in Vejby, Frederiksborg, Denmark.

25. **Bertha NIELSDATTER**-141 was born about 1771 in Vejby, Frederiksborg, Denmark. She died in 1814.

26. **Hans CHRISTENSEN**-142 was born about 1754 in Tågerup, Ramløse, Frederiksborg, Denmark. He was christened in Tågerup, Ramløse, Frederiksborg, Denmark. He died on 20 Aug 1814 in Tågerup, Ramløse, Frederiksborg, Denmark. He was buried on 29 Sep 1814 in Frederiksborg, Denmark. Hans married (MRIN:72) Susanne LARSDATTER-143 about 1776 in Taagerup, Ramlose, Frederiksborg, Denmark.

27. **Susanne LARSDATTER**-143 was born about 1748 in Ramløse, Frederiksborg, Denmark. She was christened in Ågerup, Helsinge, Frederiksborg, Denmark. She died on 20 Feb 1819. She was buried on 3 Mar 1819 in Ramløse, Frederiksborg, Denmark.

28. **Niels LARSEN**-144 was born on 5 Jun 1757 in Håre, Tanderup, Båg, Odense, Denmark. He was christened on 5 Jun 1757 in Tanderup, Odense, Denmark. He died on 14 Mar 1846 in Husby, Husby, Vends, Odense, Denmark. He was buried on 19 Mar 1846 in Husby, Odense, Denmark. Niels married (MRIN:73) Maren HANSDATTER-145.

29. **Maren HANSDATTER**-145 was born in 1769. She died before 1834.

30. **Hans SORENSEN**-146 was christened on 17 Jun 1759 in Vejlby, Odense, Denmark. He died on 26 Mar 1849 in Kindstrup, Gelsted, Odense, Denmark. He was buried on 3 Apr 1849 in Gelsted, Odense, Denmark. Hans married (MRIN:74) Kirsten MADSEN-147 on 29 Apr 1791 in Kindstrup, Gelsted, Odense, Denmark.

31. **Kirsten MADSEN**-147 was born on 20 Nov 1768 in Gelsted, Odense, Denmark. She was christened on 20 Nov 1768 in Gelsted, Odense, Denmark. She died on 19 Oct 1837 in Gelsted, Odense, Denmark. She was buried on 26 Oct 1837 in Kindstrup, Gelsted, Odense, Denmark.

Sixth Generation

32. **John GOODSALL**-284 was born on 8 Mar 1710 in Ewhurst, Sussex, England. He was christened on 23 Mar 1710 in Ewhurst, Sussex, England. He died. He was buried on 22 May 1764 in Ewhurst, Sussex, England. John married (MRIN:147) Ann JOBLIN-285 on 15 Jul 1733 in St James the Great Church, Ewhurst, Sussex, England.

33. **Ann JOBLIN**-285 was born in 1712 in Northumberland, England. She was christened in 1724. She died in 1758 in Ewhurst, Sussex, England. She was buried on 23 Sep 1758 in St James, Ewhurst,

Sussex, England.

34. **John GLOVER-288** was born about 1723 in Bodiam, Sussex, England, United Kingdom. He was christened on 23 Oct 1715 in Salehurst, Sussex, England, United Kingdom. He died on 23 Nov 1748. John married (MRIN:149) Mary BLUNDELL-289 about 1740 in Bodiam, Sussex, England.

35. **Mary BLUNDELL-289** was born about 1722 in Bodiam, Sussex, England, United Kingdom. She died.

36. **James BOOTES-290** was born on 21 May 1699 in Burwash, Sussex, England. He was christened on 21 May 1699 in Burwash, Sussex, England. He died on 13 Aug 1741 in Bodiam, Sussex, England. He was buried on 13 Aug 1741 in Bodiam, Sussex, England. James married (MRIN:150) Anne COLLINS-291 on 26 Dec 1721 in Bodiam, Sussex, England.

37. **Anne COLLINS-291** was born on 4 Nov 1693 in Bodiam, Sussex, England. She was christened on 4 Nov 1693 in Bodiam, Sussex, England. She died after 1736 in Bodiam, Sussex, England.

40. **John BALLARD-292** was born on 2 Mar 1714 in Tenterden, Kent, England. He was christened on 2 Mar 1714 in Tenterden, Kent, England, United Kingdom. He died on 14 Nov 1776 in Suffolk, England. John married (MRIN:151) Elizabeth HALLADAY-293 on 22 May 1752 in Battle, Sussex, England.

41. **Elizabeth HALLADAY-293** was born in 1731 in Catsfield, Sussex, England. She died on 15 Apr 1764 in Catsfield, Sussex, England.

42. **Thomas RELFE-294** died. Thomas married (MRIN:152) Mary-295.

43. **Mary-295** died.

44. **Edward HOBDEN-300** was born on 27 Aug 1732 in Maresfield, Sussex, England. He died on 24 Dec 1808 in Maresfield, Sussex, England. Edward married (MRIN:155) Ann BERWICK-301 on 23 Apr 1758 in Maresfield, Sussex, England.

45. **Ann BERWICK-301** was born about 1728 in Maresfield, Sussex, England. She died in 1806.

48. **Christopher JENSEN-302** was born in 1735 in Tibirke, Tibirke, Frederiksborg, Denmark. He died. Christopher married (MRIN:156) Kirsten HANSDATTER-303.

49. **Kirsten HANSDATTER-303** was born in 1735 in Tibirke, Tibirke, Frederiksborg, Denmark. She died.

50. **Niels LARSEN-305** was born in 1717 in Denmark. He died. Niels married (MRIN:158) Birthe CHRISTIANSDATTER-306.

51. **Birthe CHRISTIANSDATTER-306** was born about 1731 in Vejby, Frederiksborg, Denmark. She died in Denmark.

52. **Christen NIELSEN-308** was born about 1705 in Tågerup, Ramløse, Frederiksborg, Denmark. He died. Christen married (MRIN:160) Kirsten HANSEN-309 about 1733 in Tangerup, Ramlose, Fredriksborg, Denmark.

53. **Kirsten HANSEN-309** was born about 1709 in Tågerup, Ramløse, Frederiksborg, Denmark. She died.

54. **Lars JORGENSEN-310** was born about 1733 in Ramløse, Frederiksborg, Denmark. He died. Lars married (MRIN:161) Pernille MADSDATTER-311 in <1761> in Aagerup, Ramlose, Frederiksborg, Denmark.

55. **Pernille MADSDATTER-311** was born about 1737 in Ramløse, Frederiksborg, Denmark. She died.

56. **Lars HANSEN-312** was born about 1731 in Husby, Vends, Odense, Denmark. He died.

60. **Soren PEDERSEN-313** was born on 10 May 1722 in Vejlby, Odense, Denmark. He was christened

on 10 May 1722 in Vejlby, Odense, Denmark. He died on 25 May 1798 in Gelsted, Odense, Denmark. He was buried on 25 May 1798 in Gelsted, Odense, Denmark. Soren married (MRIN:163) Mette Sophie HANSEN-314 on 12 Sep 1755 in Rogle Molle, Vejlby, Odense, Denmark.

61. **Mette Sophie HANSEN**-314 was born about 1720 in Vejlby, Odense, Denmark. She was christened on 16 Feb 1721 in Middelfart, Odense, Denmark. She died on 13 Sep 1793 in Kindstrup, Gelsted, Odense, Denmark. She was buried on 13 Sep 1793 in Kindstrup, Gelsted, Odense, Denmark.

62. **Mads LAURITZSEN**-315 was born about 1736 in Gelsted, Odense, Denmark. He died on 19 Aug 1818 in Gelsted, Odense, Denmark. He was buried on 27 Aug 1818 in Gelsted, Odense, Denmark. Mads married (MRIN:164) Anne Catrine MADSDATTER-316 on 7 Apr 1762 in Gamborg, Odense, Denmark.

63. **Anne Catrine MADSDATTER**-316 was born in 1737 in Skaade, Aarhus, Denmark. She was christened in Denmark. She died on 7 Jun 1790 in Gelsted, Odense, Denmark. She was buried on 7 Jun 1790 in Gelsted, Odense, Denmark.

Seventh Generation

64. **James GUTSALL**-555 was christened on 16 Feb 1672 in Ewhurst, Sussex, England. He died. He was buried on 24 Apr 1740 in Ewhurst, Sussex, England. James married (MRIN:296) Ann BACKWELL-556 on 19 Oct 1697 in Ewhurst, Sussex, England.

65. **Ann BACKWELL**-556 was christened on 7 May 1676 in Ewhurst, Sussex, England. She died. She was buried in 1730 in Westfield, Sussex, England, United Kingdom.

66. **JOBLING**-557 died. JOBLING married (MRIN:297) Mrs. Joblin-558.

67. **Mrs. Joblin**-558 was born about 1685 in England, United Kingdom. She died.

68. **Robert GLOVER**-563 was born about 1689 in Salehurst, Sussex, England. He died. Robert married (MRIN:301) Elizabeth-564 about 1714 in Salehurst, Sussex, England.

69. **Elizabeth**-564 was born about 1693 in Salehurst, Sussex, England. She died.

72. **James BOOTES**-565 was born on 13 Jun 1645 in Burwash, Sussex, England, United Kingdom. He was christened on 13 Jun 1645 in Burwash, Sussex, England. He died on 13 May 1705 in Burwash, Sussex, England. He was buried on 13 May 1705 in Burwash, Sussex, England. James married (MRIN:302) Susanna-566 about 1698 in Burwash, Sussex, England.

73. **Susanna**-566 was born about 1647 in Sussex, England. She died.

74. **William COLLINS**-567 was born on 5 Jun 1672 in Bodiam, Sussex, England. He was christened on 7 Jun 1672 in Burwash, Sussex, England. He died. He was buried on 13 Apr 1720. William married (MRIN:303) Susanna SMERSWELL-568 on 1 Jul 1690 in Bodiam, Sussex, England.

75. **Susanna SMERSWELL**-568 was born in 1661 in Bodiam, Sussex, England, United Kingdom. She was christened on 1 Feb 1661 in Bodiam, Sussex, England, United Kingdom. She died.

80. **John BALLARD**-569 was born in 1683 in Tenterden, Kent, England. He was christened on 2 Mar 1683 in Tenterden, Kent, England. He died on 4 Aug 1752 in Tenterden, Kent, England. He was buried on 4 Aug 1752 in Tenterden, Kent, England. John married (MRIN:304) Margaret STEVENS-570.

81. **Margaret STEVENS**-570 was born in 1684 in Kent, England. She died.

88. **Thomas HOBDEN**-571 was born in 1700 in Sussex, England, United Kingdom. He died on 16 Jan 1768 in Maresfield, Sussex, England. Thomas married (MRIN:305) Catherine HUMPHREY-572 on

5 Dec 1725 in St Ann, Lewes, Sussex, England.

89. **Catherine HUMPHREY**-572 was born in 1700 in Sussex, England, United Kingdom. She died.

90. **Thomas BERWICK**-573 was born in 1700 in Sussex, England. He died in Jul 1770 in Buxted, Sussex, England. He was buried on 6 Jul 1770 in Buxted, Buxted, Sussex, England. Thomas married (MRIN:306) Lucy GLAZIER-574 on 15 Jun 1728 in Buxted, Sussex, England.

91. **Lucy GLAZIER**-574 was born in 1704 in Buxted, Sussex, England. She died in Sep 1767 in Buxted, Sussex, England.

96. **Jens**-575 was born in 1710 in Vejby, Frederiksborg, Denmark. He died.

98. **Hans**-576 was born in 1710 in Tibirke, Tibirke, Frederiksborg, Denmark. He died.

100. **Lars**-577 was born in 1695 in Vejby, Vejby, Frederiksborg, Denmark. He died.

102. **Christians**-578 was born in 1705 in Vejby, Vejby, Frederiksborg, Denmark. He died. Christians married (MRIN:310) Nelie-579.

103. **Nelie**-579 was born in 1705 in Vejby, Frederiksborg, Denmark. She died.

104. **Niels**-580 was born in 1680 in Tågerup, Ramløse, Frederiksborg, Denmark. He died. Niels married (MRIN:311) Karen-581.

105. **Karen**-581 was born in 1680 in Tågerup, Ramløse, Frederiksborg, Denmark. She died.

106. **Hans**-582 was born in 1685 in Tågerup, Ramløse, Frederiksborg, Denmark. He died. Hans married (MRIN:312) Maren-583.

107. **Maren**-583 was born in 1685 in Tågerup, Ramløse, Frederiksborg, Denmark. She died.

108. **Jorgens**-584 was born in 1710 in Ramløse, Frederiksborg, Denmark. He died. Jorgens married (MRIN:313) Johanne-585.

109. **Johanne**-585 was born in 1710 in Ramløse, Frederiksborg, Denmark. She died.

110. **Mads**-586 was born in 1710 in Ramløse, Frederiksborg, Denmark. He died. Mads married (MRIN:314) Susanne-587.

111. **Susanne**-587 was born in 1710 in Ramløse, Frederiksborg, Denmark. She died.

120. **Peder TERCHELSEN**-588 was born in 1675 in Røjle, Vejlby Sogn, Vends Herred, Odense Amt, Denmark. He was christened on 25 Nov 1677 in Vejlby Kirke, Vejlby Sogn, Vends Herred, Odense Amt, Denmark. He died in 1740 in Røjle, Vejlby Sogn, Vends Herred, Odense Amt, Denmark. He was buried on 12 Jul 1740 in Vejlby Kirke, Vejlby Sogn, Vends Herred, Odense Amt, Denmark. Peder married (MRIN:315) Bodil RASMUSDATTER-589 on 27 Jun 1706 in Vejlby Kirke, Vejlby Sogn, Vends Herred, Odense Amt, Denmark.

121. **Bodil RASMUSDATTER**-589 was born in 1680. She died. She was buried in 1726.

122. **Hans ANDERSEN**-590 was born about 1695. He died. Hans married (MRIN:316) Maren POVELSEN-591.

123. **Maren POVELSEN**-591 was born about 1694 in Middelfart, Odense, Denmark. She died on 19 Jun 1753 in Vejlby, Odense, Denmark. She was buried on 19 Jun 1753 in Vejlby, Odense, Denmark.

124. **Lauritz MADSEN**-592 was born in 1705 in Strandby, Ålborg, Denmark. He died. Lauritz married (MRIN:317) Mette JENSEN-593 on 24 May 1744 in Strandby, Aalborg, Denmark.

125. **Mette JENSEN**-593 was born on 7 Apr 1713 in Ullits, Ålborg, Denmark. She was christened on 14 May 1713 in Ullits, Ålborg, Denmark. She died on 11 Mar 1761 in Ullits, Ålborg, Denmark. She was buried on 11 Mar 1761 in Strandby, Ålborg, Denmark.

126. **Mads PEDERSEN**-594 was born in 1693 in Skaade, Aarhus, Denmark. He died on 23 Nov 1755 in Skaade, Aarhus, Denmark. He was buried on 23 Nov 1755 in Skaade, Aarhus, Denmark. Mads married (MRIN:318) Anne Cathrine RASMUSDATTER-595 on 14 Nov 1728 in Beder, Aarhus, Denmark.

127. **Anne Cathrine RASMUSDATTER**-595 was born in 1700 in Beder, Aarhus, Denmark. She died on 28 Nov 1762. She was buried on 28 Nov 1762 in Skaade, Aarhus, Denmark.

Eighth Generation

128. **Thomas GUTSELL**-1012 was born on 13 Sep 1621 in Ewhurst, Sussex, England. He was christened on 4 Apr 1620 in Ticehurst, Sussex, England. He died on 27 Feb 1680 in Ewhurst, Sussex, England. He was buried on 27 Feb 1680 in Ewhurst, Sussex, England. Thomas married (MRIN:557) Elizabeth FREEMAN-1013 in 1653 in Ewhurst, Sussex, England.

129. **Elizabeth FREEMAN**-1013 was born in 1632 in Ewhurst, Sussex, England, United Kingdom. She died in 1701 in Ewhurst, Sussex, England, United Kingdom. She was buried on 3 Feb 1701 in Ewhurst, Sussex, England.

130. **Henry BLACKWELL**-1015 was christened on 16 Sep 1632 in Rudgwick, Sussex, England. He died. He was buried on 9 Jul 1679 in Ewhurst, Sussex, England. Henry married (MRIN:559) Judith LAKER-1016 on 26 Nov 1668 in Wadhurst, Sussex, England.

131. **Judith LAKER**-1016 was christened on 11 Mar 1637 in Wadhurst, Sussex, England. She died. She was buried on 29 May 1704 in Ewhurst, Sussex, England.

144. **James BOOTES**-1020 was born on 10 May 1608 in Etchingham, Sussex, England. He was christened on 1 May 1608 in Etchingham, Sussex, England. He died on 24 Oct 1667 in Burwash, Sussex, England. He was buried on 24 Oct 1667 in Burwash, Sussex, England. James married (MRIN:562) Anne WENHAM-1021 on 27 Oct 1634 in Burwash, Sussex, England.

145. **Anne WENHAM**-1021 was born on 2 Oct 1608 in Chalvington, Sussex, England. She was christened on 2 Oct 1608 in Chalvington, Sussex, England, United Kingdom. She died in 1681 in Sussex, England, United Kingdom.

148. **Thomas COLLINS**-1022 was born about 1644 in Burwash, Sussex, England. He was christened on 2 Mar 1644 in Hamsey, Sussex, England. He died. Thomas married (MRIN:563) Margaret-1023 about 1670 in of Burwash, Sussex, England.

149. **Margaret**-1023 was born about 1649 in Burwash, Sussex, England, United Kingdom. She was christened about 1649 in England, United Kingdom. She died.

150. **William SMERSWELL**-1024 was born about 1630 in Bodiam, Sussex, England, United Kingdom. He was christened on 12 Dec 1630 in Bodiam, Sussex, England, United Kingdom. He died. He was buried on 19 Feb 1702 in Bodiam, Sussex, England, United Kingdom. William married (MRIN:564) Ann BAKER-1025 on 22 Oct 1654 in Bodiam, Sussex, England.

151. **Ann BAKER**-1025 was born about 1633 in Bodiam, Sussex, England, United Kingdom. She was christened on 12 Dec 1630 in Bodiam, Sussex, England, United Kingdom. She died. She was buried on 7 Mar 1691 in Bodiam, Sussex, England, United Kingdom.

162. **Ferdinando STEPHENS**-1026 was born in 1628. He died on 1 Jun 1703 in Kent, England. Ferdinando married (MRIN:565) Jane MORRIS-1027 on 9 Feb 1669 in Kent, England.

163. **Jane MORRIS**-1027 was christened on 8 Feb 1637 in Benenden, Kent, England. She died on 28 Feb 1716 in Kent, England.

176. **William HOBDEN**-1028 was born on 4 Mar 1664 in Chailey, Barcombe, Sussex, England. He was christened on 3 Apr 1664 in Barcombe, Sussex, England. He died on 25 May 1734 in Sussex, England. William married (MRIN:567) Mary BRIGHTRIDGE-1029 on 29 May 1696.

177. **Mary BRIGHTRIDGE**-1029 was born about 1668 in Barcombe, Sussex, England. She was christened on 13 Sep 1668 in Barcombe, Sussex, England. She died on 3 Jun 1712 in Sussex, England.

182. **John GLAZIER**-1030 was born in 1682 in England. He died in England. John married (MRIN:568) Elizabeth DURRANT-1031 about 1702 in England.

183. **Elizabeth DURRANT**-1031 was born in 1684 in England. She was christened on 14 Oct 1684 in Tingewick, Buckinghamshire, England, United Kingdom. She died in England.

240. **Terchel PEDERSEN**-1032 was born about 1644 in of Roile, Vejlby, Denmark. He died in 1713 in Røjle, Vejlby Sogn, Vends Herred, Odense Amt, Denmark. He was buried on 4 Oct 1713 in Vejlby Kirke, Vejlby Sogn, Vends Herred, Odense Amt, Denmark.

246. **Poufvel ANDERSEN**-1033 was christened on 17 Jan 1664 in Indslev, Odense, Denmark. He died. He was buried on 3 May 1724 in Middelfart, Odense, Denmark. Poufvel married (MRIN:570) Anne HANSEN-1034.

247. **Anne HANSEN**-1034 died. She was buried on 5 Jan 1736 in Middelfart, Odense, Denmark.

250. **Jens CHRISTENSEN**-1035 was born in <1695> in Aalborg, Denmark. He died. Jens married (MRIN:571) Annie NIELSDATTER-1036 in <1720> in Gunderup, Aalborg, Denmark.

251. **Annie NIELSDATTER**-1036 was born in <1699> in Aalborg, Denmark. She died.

252. **Peder LAURSEN**-1039 was born about 1661 in Sønderup, Sorø, Denmark. He died in Apr 1736 in Skaade, Aarhus, Denmark. Peder married (MRIN:573) Mrs. Peder LAURSEN-1040 about 1681 in Of Skaade, Holme, Aarhus, Denmark.

253. **Mrs. Peder LAURSEN**-1040 was born about 1665 in Fana, Hordaland, Norway. She died.

254. **Rasmus**-1041 was born about 1674 in Fulden, Beder, Århus, Denmark. He died. Rasmus married (MRIN:574) Mrs- Rasmus-1042 about 1694 in Of Fulden, Beder, Aarhus, Denmark.

255. **Mrs- Rasmus**-1042 was born about 1676 in Fulden, Beder, Århus, Denmark. She died.

Ninth Generation

256. **Thomas GUDSALL**-1140 was born in 1591 in Frant, Sussex, England. He died in 1629 in Sedlescombe, Sussex, , England. Thomas married (MRIN:646) Grace BROOKER-1141.

257. **Grace BROOKER**-1141 was born in 1584 in of Lamberhurst, Kent, England. She died. She was buried on 18 Apr 1624 in Brenchley, Kent, England.

260. **Humfry BLACKWELL**-1151 was born about 1600 in Sussex, England, United Kingdom. He was christened on 15 Dec 1590 in Slinfold, West Sussex, England. He died. Humfry married (MRIN:653) Agnis COMBER-1152 on 29 Sep 1617 in Rudgwick, Sussex, England.

261. **Agnis COMBER**-1152 was born about 1600 in England, United Kingdom. She died.

262. **Thomas LAKER**-1193 was born about 1609 in Wadhurst, Sussex, England, United Kingdom. He died. He was buried on 30 Dec 1680 in Wadhurst, Sussex, England. Thomas married (MRIN:676) Judith HUES-1194 on 11 Aug 1634 in Wadhurst, Sussex, England.

263. **Judith HUES**-1194 was born about 1613 in Wadhurst, Sussex, England, United Kingdom. She died.

She was buried on 23 Jul 1678 in Wadhurst, Sussex, England.

288. **Richard BOOTES**-1202 was born about 1578 in Etchingham, Sussex, England. He died on 30 May 1633 in Sussex, England. He was buried on 30 May 1633 in Etchingham, Etchingham, Sussex, England. Richard married (MRIN:681) Elinor-1203 about 1603 in Of Etchingham, Sussex, England.

289. **Elinor**-1203 was born about 1582 in Etchingham, Sussex, England, United Kingdom. She died.

290. **William WENHAM**-1210 was born on 23 Oct 1569 in Iden, Sussex, England. He was christened on 23 Oct 1569 in Iden, Sussex, England, United Kingdom. He died. William married (MRIN:685) Anne SAINTGEORGE-1211 on 20 Jan 1608 in Chalvington, Sussex, England, United Kingdom.

291. **Anne SAINTGEORGE**-1211 was born in 1570 in Chalvington, Sussex, England. She died.

296. **COLLINS**-1219 was born about 1610 in England, United Kingdom. He died. COLLINS married (MRIN:690) Mrs. Collins-1220 about 1640 in England.

297. **Mrs. Collins**-1220 was born about 1615 in England, United Kingdom. She died.

300. **John SMERSALL the Third**-1221 was born about 1604 in Bodiam, Sussex, England, United Kingdom. He died. He was buried on 25 Apr 1648 in Bodiam, Sussex, England, United Kingdom. John married (MRIN:691) Dorothy BOORNE OR BOURNE-1222 on 7 Aug 1629 in Bodiam, Sussex, England.

301. **Dorothy BOORNE OR BOURNE**-1222 was born about 1608 in Bodiam, Sussex, England, United Kingdom. She was christened on 3 Feb 1610 in Bodiam, Sussex, England, United Kingdom. She died.

302. **BAKER**-1266 was born about 1600 in England, United Kingdom. He died. BAKER married (MRIN:726) Mrs. Baker-1267 about 1630 in England.

303. **Mrs. Baker**-1267 was born about 1603 in England, United Kingdom. She died.

326. **John MORRIS**-1268 was born about 1615 in Kent, England. He died. John married (MRIN:727) Anne-1269.

327. **Anne**-1269 died.

352. **Thomas HOBDEN**-1271 was born about 1634 in Hamsey, Sussex, England, United Kingdom. He died. Thomas married (MRIN:729) Jane PARKER-1272 on 19 May 1663 in Hamsey, Sussex, England.

353. **Jane PARKER**-1272 was born in 1639 in England. She died in 1728 in Sussex, England.

354. **John BRIGHTRIDGE**-1293 was born about 1648 in Barcombe, Sussex, England. He died. John married (MRIN:744) Ellinor CARMAN-1294 about 1666 in Barcombe, Sussex, England.

355. **Ellinor CARMAN**-1294 was born about 1652 in Barcombe, Sussex, England. She died.

366. **Ambrose DURRANT**-1295 died.

480. **Peder**-1296 was born about 1630. He died.

492. **Anders POUFVELSEN**-1297 died.

504. **_____ Laurs...**-1298 was born about 1636 in Skaade, Aarhus, Denmark. He died. _____ married (MRIN:748) Mrs. Laurs-1299 about 1667 in Of Skaade, Holme, Aarhus, Denmark.

505. **Mrs. Laurs**-1299 was born about 1640 in Of Skaade, Holme, Denmark. She died.

Tenth Generation

512. **John GOODSALL**-1146 was born in 1572 in England. He died. John married (MRIN:650) Elizabeth DEPRON-1147 in 1590 in Frant, Sussex, England.

513. **Elizabeth DEPRON**-1147 was born in 1572 in England. She died.

520. **Humfrey BLACKWELL**-1153 was born about 1570 in England, United Kingdom. He died. Humfrey married (MRIN:654) Mrs. Blackwell-1154 about 1590 in England.

521. **Mrs. Blackwell**-1154 was born about 1575 in England, United Kingdom. She died.

522. **John COMBER**-1155 was born about 1572 in Brighton, Sussex, England. He was christened on 15 Oct 1572 in Brighton, Sussex, England. He died in Oct 1625 in Brighton, Sussex, England. He was buried on 5 Nov 1625 in Brighton, Sussex, England, United Kingdom. John married (MRIN:655) Leatyce GUNN-1156 on 17 Oct 1591 in St. Nicholas Parish, Brighton, Sussex, England.

523. **Leatyce GUNN**-1156 was christened on 2 Apr 1570 in Brighton, Sussex, England, United Kingdom. She died.

524. **William LAKER**-1195 was born in 1585 in Wadhurst, Sussex, England. He died. William married (MRIN:677) Mrs. Mary LAKER-1196 about 1608 in Sussex, England.

525. **Mrs. Mary LAKER**-1196 was born in 1585 in Wadhurst, Sussex, England. She died.

526. **HUES**-1198 was born about 1585 in England, United Kingdom. He died. HUES married (MRIN:679) Mrs. Hues-1199 about 1610 in England.

527. **Mrs. Hues**-1199 was born about 1590 in England, United Kingdom. She died.

576. **Richard BOOTES**-1204 was born about 1550 in Sussex, England, United Kingdom. He died. Richard married (MRIN:682) Elizabeth ROLF-1205 in Jun 1571 in East Grinstead, Sussex, England.

577. **Elizabeth ROLF**-1205 was born about 1555 in East Grinstead, Sussex, England. She died.

580. **Hugh WENAM**-1212 was born in 1550 in Iden, Sussex, England, United Kingdom. He died. Hugh married (MRIN:686) Eve WILLES-1213 on 25 Jun 1571 in Iden, Sussex, England.

581. **Eve WILLES**-1213 was born in 1550 in Iden, Sussex, England, United Kingdom. She died.

582. **Mr. SAINTGEORGE**-1214 was born in 1548 in Chalvington, Sussex, England. He died in England. Mr. SAINTGEORGE married (MRIN:687) Mrs. SAINTGEORGE-1215.

583. **Mrs. SAINTGEORGE**-1215 was born in 1548 in Chalvington, Sussex, England. She died in England.

600. **John SMERSALL**-1223 was born about 1568 in Brede, Sussex, England, United Kingdom. He died. He was buried on 16 Oct 1657 in Bodiam, Sussex, England, United Kingdom. John married (MRIN:692) Margaret CHESMAN-1224 on 11 Jun 1593 in Brede, Sussex, England.

601. **Margaret CHESMAN**-1224 was born in 1575 in Brede, Sussex, England, United Kingdom. She was christened on 13 Feb 1575 in Brede, Sussex, England, United Kingdom. She died. She was buried on 28 Oct 1658 in Bodiam, Sussex, England, United Kingdom.

602. **Robert BOURNE**-1225 was born about 1570 in Bodiam, Sussex, England, United Kingdom. He was christened on 5 Oct 1561 in Bobbingworth, Essex, England, United Kingdom. He died on 28 Feb 1605 in England, United Kingdom. He was buried on 24 Oct 1650 in Bodiam, Sussex, England, United Kingdom. Robert married (MRIN:693) Susan MOORE-1226 about 1593 in Bodian, , Sussex, England.

603. **Susan MOORE**-1226 was born about 1574 in Rye, Sussex, England, United Kingdom. She was christened on 20 May 1576 in Sandhurst, Kent, England. She died on 29 Jan 1645. She was buried

on 29 Jan 1645 in Bodiam, Sussex, England, United Kingdom.

652. **John MORRIS**-1270 was born about 1590 in Kent, England. He died.

704. **William HOBDEN**-1273 was born in 1597 in Sussex, England. He died in England. William married (MRIN:730) Agnes GEERAT-1274 on 21 Nov 1621 in Crowhurst, Sussex, England.

705. **Agnes GEERAT**-1274 died in England.

706. **John PARKER**-1275 was born on 3 May 1617 in Erwarton, Suffolk, England, United Kingdom. He died. John married (MRIN:731) Judith TREE-1276 in 1638 in England.

707. **Judith TREE**-1276 was born in 1617 in Sussex, England. She died in Sussex, England.

Eleventh Generation

1024. **GOODSALL**-1150 was born in 1550 in Frant, Sussex, England. He died.

1044. **Leonard COMBER**-1157 was born about 1534 in Brighton, Sussex, England. He died in Feb 1579 in Brighton, Sussex, England. Leonard married (MRIN:656) Margaret FARNCOMBE-1158 on 25 Feb 1565 in Saint Nicholas, Brighton, Sussex, England.

1045. **Margaret FARNCOMBE**-1158 was born about 1540 in Patcham, Sussex, England. She died.

1046. **Richard GUNN**-1159 was born about 1548 in Brighton, Sussex, England, United Kingdom. He died. Richard married (MRIN:657) Marie-1160 about 1569 in of Brighton, Sussex, England.

1047. **Marie**-1160 was born about 1548 in Brighton, Sussex, England, United Kingdom. She died. She was buried on 22 Dec 1606 in Brighton, Sussex, England, United Kingdom.

1152. **Mr. BOOTS OR BOOTES**-1206 was born in 1528 in Sussex, England. He died in England. Mr. BOOTS OR BOOTES married (MRIN:683) Mrs. BOOTS OR BOOTES-1207.

1153. **Mrs. BOOTS OR BOOTES**-1207 was born in 1528 in Sussex, England. She died in England.

1154. **Mr. ROLF**-1208 was born in 1533 in East Grinstead, Sussex, England. He died in England. Mr. ROLF married (MRIN:684) Mrs. ROLF-1209.

1155. **Mrs. ROLF**-1209 was born in 1533 in Greenstead, Essex, England. She died in England.

1160. **Mr. WENAM**-1216 was born in 1528 in Sussex, England. He died in England. Mr. WENAM married (MRIN:688) Mrs. WENAM-1217.

1161. **Mrs. WENAM**-1217 was born in 1528 in Iden, Sussex, England. She died in England.

1162. **Richard WILLES**-1218 was born in 1520 in Iden, Sussex, England. He died on 5 May 1563 in Iden, Sussex, England.

1200. **John SMERSALL**-1228 was born about 1538 in Brede, Sussex, England, United Kingdom. He died. He was buried on 13 Apr 1606 in Brede, Sussex, England, United Kingdom. John married (MRIN:695) Bedreas PRETTLE-1229 about 1565 in England.

1201. **Bedreas PRETTLE**-1229 died on 19 Nov 1592.

1202. **Georgii CHESMAN**-1232 was born about 1540 in Brede, Sussex, England, United Kingdom. He died. Georgii married (MRIN:697) Bridget COOPER-1233 on 2 Dec 1570 in Burwash, Sussex, England.

1203. **Bridget COOPER**-1233 was born about 1543 in Brede, Sussex, England, United Kingdom. She died after 1593.

1204. **William BOURNE**-1234 was born about 1527 in Bobbingworth, Essex, England. He died on 29 Apr 1591 in Bobbingworth, Essex, England, United Kingdom. William married (MRIN:698) Margaret RYSE-1235.

1205. **Margaret RYSE**-1235 was born in 1531 in Potter Newton, Yorkshire, England. She was christened in 1531 in St Michael, Cornhill, London, England. She died on 28 Dec 1594 in Bobbingworth, Essex, England, United Kingdom.

1206. **William MOORE**-1244 was born about 1537 in Sandhurst, Kent, England. He died. William married (MRIN:709) Mrs William MOORE-1245 about 1562 in of Sandhurst, Kent, England.

1207. **Mrs William MOORE**-1245 was born about 1541 in Sandhurst, Kent, England. She died.

1408. **Adam HOBDEN**-1277 was born in 1569 in Alfriston, Sussex, England. He died on 8 Dec 1613 in England. Adam married (MRIN:732) Margaret WALKER-1278 in 1595 in Alfriston, Sussex, England.

1409. **Margaret WALKER**-1278 was born in 1574 in Alfriston, Sussex, England. She died in 1633 in England.

Twelfth Generation

2088. **William COMBER**-1163 was born about 1503 in of Brighton, Sussex, England. He died. William married (MRIN:659) Mrs. William COMBER-1164.

2089. **Mrs. William COMBER**-1164 was born about 1507 in Brighton, Sussex, England. She died.

2090. **Richard FARNCOMBE**-1166 was born about 1514 in Patcham, Sussex, England. He died in Jul 1564 in Patcham, Sussex, England. He was buried on 29 Jul 1564. Richard married (MRIN:661) Juliana-1167 in 1534 in Patcham, Sussex, England.

2091. **Juliana**-1167 was born about 1520 in Patcham, Sussex, England. She died in Oct 1563 in Patcham, Sussex, England.

2400. **SMERSALL**-1246 was born about 1510 in England, United Kingdom. He died. SMERSALL married (MRIN:710) Mrs. Smersall-1247 about 1535 in England.

2401. **Mrs. Smersall**-1247 was born about 1515 in England, United Kingdom. She died.

2406. **William COOPER**-1248 was born about 1523 in Brede, Sussex, England. He died. William married (MRIN:711) Mrs William COOPER-1249 about 1548 in of Brede, Sussex, England.

2407. **Mrs William COOPER**-1249 was born about 1527 in Brede, Sussex, England. She died.

2408. **John BOURNE**-1250 was born in 1500 in Bobbingworth, Essex, England. He died in 1561 in Bobbingworth, Essex, England. John married (MRIN:712) Margaret-1251 in 1525 in Bobbingworth, , Essex, England.

2409. **Margaret**-1251 was born in 1505 in Bobbingworth, Essex, England. She died in 1564 in England.

2410. **Richard RYSE**-1259 was born in 1504 in Bedford, Bedfordshire, England, United Kingdom. He died about 1539 in Bedfordshire, England. Richard married (MRIN:720) Mrs Richard RYSE-1260 about 1529 in Of, Bedford, England.

2411. **Mrs Richard RYSE**-1260 was born in 1507 in Bedford, Bedfordshire, England, United Kingdom. She died in 1536/1595.

2816. **James HOBDEN**-1279 was born in 1545 in Sussex, England. He died in 1570 in England. James married (MRIN:733) Petronella-1280.

2817. **Petronella**-1280 was born in England. She died in England.

2818. **William WALKER**-1281 died.

Thirteenth Generation

4816. **Walter BOURNE OR BORNE**-1264 was born about 1474 in Wick, Worcestershire, England. He died after 1532 in Worcestershire, England.

5632. **Thomas HOBDEN**-1282 was born in 1520 in Sussex, England. He died in 1568 in England. Thomas married (MRIN:736) Hannah Petrenella POSKITT-1283.

5633. **Hannah Petrenella POSKITT**-1283 was born in 1520 in Drax, Yorkshire, England. She died in 1837 in England.

Index

Name	ID	Page
GLOVER, John (b.1723)	34	4
GLOVER, Robert (b.1689)	68	5
GLOVER, Sarah Blundell (b.1743)	17	2
GOODSALL, (b.1550)	1024	11
GOODSALL, John (b.1710)	32	3
GOODSALL, John (b.1572)	512	10
GOODSALL, Thomas (b.1734)	16	2
GOODSELL, Alfred (b.1851)	2	1
GOODSELL, John (b.1793)	4	1
GOODSELL, John (c.1767)	8	2
GOODSELL, Joseph Franklin (b.1886)	1	1
GUDSALL, Thomas (b.1591)	256	8
GUNN, Leatyce (c.1570)	523	10
GUNN, Richard (b.1548)	1046	11
GUTSALL, James (c.1672)	64	5
GUTSELL, Thomas (b.1621)	128	7
HALLADAY, Elizabeth (b.1731)	41	4
HANSDATTER, Kirsten (b.1735)	49	4
HANSDATTER, Maren (b.1769)	29	3
HANSDATTER, Pernille (b.1789)	13	2
HANSEN, Anne	247	8
HANSEN, Anne Catrine (b.1801)	15	2
HANSEN, Kirsten (b.1709)	53	4
HANSEN, Lars (b.1731)	56	4
HANSEN, Mette Sophie (b.1720)	61	5
HOBDEN, Adam (b.1569)	1408	12
HOBDEN, Edward (b.1732)	44	4
HOBDEN, James (b.1545)	2816	12
HOBDEN, Mary (b.1790)	11	2
HOBDEN, Richard (b.1756)	22	3
HOBDEN, Thomas (b.1520)	5632	13
HOBDEN, Thomas (b.1700)	88	5
HOBDEN, Thomas (b.1634)	352	9
HOBDEN, William (b.1664)	176	8
HOBDEN, William (b.1597)	704	11
HUES, (b.1585)	526	10
HUES, Judith (b.1613)	263	8
HUMPHREY, Catherine (b.1700)	89	6
JENSEN, Christopher (b.1735)	48	4
JENSEN, Hannah Christina (b.1853)	3	1
JENSEN, Hans (b.1825)	6	1
JENSEN, Mette (b.1713)	125	6
JOBLIN, Ann (b.1712)	33	3
JOBLING,	66	5
JORGENSEN, Lars (b.1733)	54	4
LAKER, Judith (c.1637)	131	7
LAKER, Mary (b.1585)	525	10
LAKER, Thomas (b.1609)	262	8
LAKER, William (b.1585)	524	10
LARSDATTER, Maren (b.1830)	7	1
LARSDATTER, Susanne (b.1748)	27	3

Name	ID	Page
LARSEN, Niels (b.1717)	50	4
LARSEN, Niels (b.1757)	28	3
LAURITZSEN, Mads (b.1736)	62	5
LAURSEN, Peder (b.1661)	252	8
LAURSEN, Peder (b.1665)	253	8
MADSDATTER, Anne C (b.1737)	63	5
MADSDATTER, Pernille (b.1737)	55	4
MADSEN, Jens (b.1799)	12	2
MADSEN, Kirsten (b.1768)	31	3
MADSEN, Lauritz (b.1705)	124	6
MOORE, Mrs William (b.1541)	1207	12
MOORE, Susan (b.1574)	603	10
MOORE, William (b.1537)	1206	12
MORRIS, Jane (c.1637)	163	7
MORRIS, John (b.1615)	326	9
MORRIS, John (b.1590)	652	11
NIELSDATTER, Annie (b.1699)	251	8
NIELSDATTER, Bertha (b.1771)	25	3
NIELSEN, Christen (b.1705)	52	4
NIELSEN, Lars (b.1793)	14	2
PARKER, Jane (b.1639)	353	9
PARKER, John (b.1617)	706	11
PEDERSEN, Mads (b.1693)	126	7
PEDERSEN, Soren (b.1722)	60	4
PEDERSEN, Terchel (b.1644)	240	8
POSKITT, Hannah P (b.1520)	5633	13
POUFVELSEN, Anders	492	9
POVELSEN, Maren (b.1694)	123	6
PRETTLE, Bedreas (d.1592)	1201	11
RASMUSDATTER, Anne C (b.1700)	127	7
RASMUSDATTER, Bodil (b.1680)	121	6
RELFE, Ann (b.1760)	21	3
RELFE, Thomas	42	4
ROLF, (b.1533)	1154	11
ROLF, (b.1533)	1155	11
ROLF, Elizabeth (b.1555)	577	10
RYSE, Margaret (b.1531)	1205	12
RYSE, Mrs Richard (b.1507)	2411	12
RYSE, Richard (b.1504)	2410	12
SAINTGEORGE, (b.1548)	582	10
SAINTGEORGE, (b.1548)	583	10
SAINTGEORGE, Anne (b.1570)	291	9
SMERSALL, (b.1510)	2400	12
SMERSALL, John the Third (b.1604)	300	9
SMERSALL, John (b.1568)	600	10
SMERSALL, John (b.1538)	1200	11
SMERSWELL, Susanna (b.1661)	75	5
SMERSWELL, William (b.1630)	150	7
SORENSEN, Hans (c.1759)	30	3
STEPHENS, Ferdinando (b.1628)	162	7
STEVENS, Margaret (b.1684)	81	5

Ancestors of Joseph Franklin GOODSELL-8

GOODSALL-1150 (b. 1550-Frant, Sussex, England d. Deceased)

John GOODSALL-1146 (b. 1572-England d. Deceased)

Thomas GUDSALL-1140 (b. 1591-Frant, Sussex, England d. 1629-Sedlescombe, Sussex, , England)

Elizabeth DEPRON-1147 (b. 1572-England d. Deceased)

Thomas GUTSELL-1012 (b. 13 Sep 1621-Ewhurst, Sussex, England d. 27 Feb 1680-Ewhurst, S, England)

Grace BROOKER-1141 (b. 1584-of Lamberhurst, Kent, England d. Deceased)

James GUTSALL-555 (r. 16 Feb 1672-Ewhurst, Sussex, England d. Deceased)

Elizabeth FREEMAN-1013 (b. 1632-Ewhurst, Sussex, E, United Kingdom d. 1701-E, S, E, United Kingdom)

John GOODSALL-284 (b. 8 Mar 1710-Ewhurst, Sussex, England d. Deceased)

Humfrey BLACKWELL-1153 (b. Abt 1570-E, United Kingdom d. Deceased)

Humfry BLACKWELL-1151 (b. Abt 1600-S, E, United Kingdom d. Deceased)

Mrs. Blackwell -1154 (b. Abt 1575-E, United Kingdom d. Deceased)

Henry BLACKWELL-1015 (r. 16 Sep 1632-Rudgwick, Sussex, England d. Deceased)

William COMBER-1163 (b. Abt 1503-of Brighton, Sussex, England d. Deceased)

Leonard COMBER-1157 (b. Abt 1534-Brighton, Sussex, England d. Feb 1579-, , England)

Mrs. William COMBER-1164 (b. Abt 1507-Brighton, Sussex, England d. Deceased)

John COMBER-1155 (b. Abt 1572-Brighton, S, England d. Oct 1625-Brighton, Sussex, England)

Richard FARNCOMBE-1166 (b. Abt 1514-Patcham, Sussex, England d. Jul 1564-)

Margaret FARNCOMBE-1158 (b. Abt 1540-Patcham, Sussex, England d. Deceased)

Juliana -1167 (b. Abt 1520-Patcham, S, England d. Oct 1563-Patcham, S, England)

Agnis COMBER-1152 (b. Abt 1600-England, United Kingdom d. Deceased)

Richard GUNN-1159 (b. Abt 1548-B, S, , United Kingdom d. Deceased)

Leatyce GUNN-1156 (r. 2 Apr 1570-B, S, , United Kingdom d. Deceased)

Marie -1160 (b. Abt 1548-B, S, E, United Kingdom d. Deceased)

Ann BACKWELL-556 (r. 7 May 1676-Ewhurst, Sussex, England d. Deceased)

William LAKER-1195 (b. 1585-Wadhurst, Sussex, England d. Deceased)

Thomas LAKER-1193 (b. Abt 1609-W, S, E, United Kingdom d. Deceased)

Mrs. Mary LAKER-1196 (b. 1585-Wadhurst, S, England d. Deceased)

Judith LAKER-1016 (r. 11 Mar 1637-Wadhurst, Sussex, England d. Deceased)

HUES-1198 (b. Abt 1585-England, United Kingdom d. Deceased)

Judith HUES-1194 (b. Abt 1613-Wadhurst, S, E, United Kingdom d. Deceased)

Mrs. Hues -1199 (b. Abt 1590-England, United Kingdom d. Deceased)

Thomas GOODSALL-132 (b. 1734-Ewhurst, Sussex, England d. 1813)

JOBLING-557 (d. Deceased)

Ann JOBLIN-285 (b. 1712-Northumberland, England d. 1758-Ewhurst, Sussex, England)

Mrs. Joblin -558 (b. Abt 1685-England, United Kingdom d. Deceased)

John GOODSELL-65 (r. 19 Jul 1767-Salehurst, Sussex, England d. 4 Oct 1840-Hastings, Sussex, England)

Robert GLOVER-563 (b. Abt 1689-Salehurst, Sussex, England d. Deceased)

John GLOVER-288 (b. Abt 1723-Bodiam, Sussex, England, United Kingdom d. 23 Nov 1748)

Elizabeth -564 (b. Abt 1693-Salehurst, Sussex, England d. Deceased)

Sarah Blundell GLOVER-133 (b. Abt 1743-Salehurst, Sussex, England, United Kingdom d. 1812)

Mary BLUNDELL-289 (b. Abt 1722-Bodiam, Sussex, England, United Kingdom d. Deceased)

John GOODSELL-32 (b. 24 Jul 1793-Hastings, Sussex, England d. 12 Sep 1855-St.Mary Magdalen, St. Leonard-On-Sea, Sussex, England)

Mr. BOOTS OR BOOTES-1206 (b. 1528-Sussex, England d. Deceased-England)

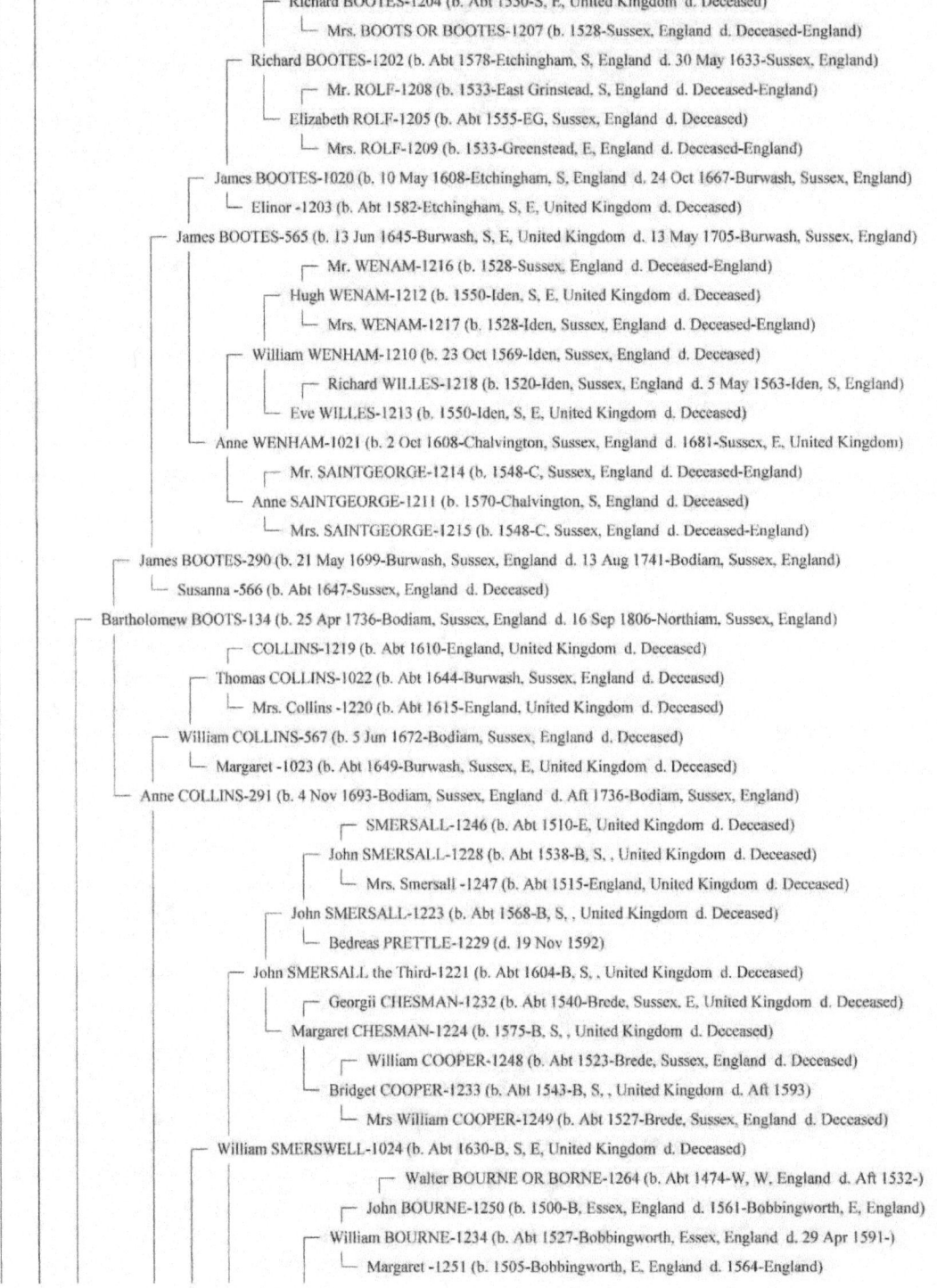

Richard BOOTES-1204 (b. Abt 1550-S, E, United Kingdom d. Deceased)
└ Mrs. BOOTS OR BOOTES-1207 (b. 1528-Sussex, England d. Deceased-England)

Richard BOOTES-1202 (b. Abt 1578-Etchingham, S, England d. 30 May 1633-Sussex, England)
┌ Mr. ROLF-1208 (b. 1533-East Grinstead, S, England d. Deceased-England)
└ Elizabeth ROLF-1205 (b. Abt 1555-EG, Sussex, England d. Deceased)
└ Mrs. ROLF-1209 (b. 1533-Greenstead, E, England d. Deceased-England)

James BOOTES-1020 (b. 10 May 1608-Etchingham, S, England d. 24 Oct 1667-Burwash, Sussex, England)
└ Elinor -1203 (b. Abt 1582-Etchingham, S, E, United Kingdom d. Deceased)

James BOOTES-565 (b. 13 Jun 1645-Burwash, S, E, United Kingdom d. 13 May 1705-Burwash, Sussex, England)
┌ Mr. WENAM-1216 (b. 1528-Sussex, England d. Deceased-England)
Hugh WENAM-1212 (b. 1550-Iden, S, E, United Kingdom d. Deceased)
└ Mrs. WENAM-1217 (b. 1528-Iden, Sussex, England d. Deceased-England)

William WENHAM-1210 (b. 23 Oct 1569-Iden, Sussex, England d. Deceased)
┌ Richard WILLES-1218 (b. 1520-Iden, Sussex, England d. 5 May 1563-Iden, S, England)
Eve WILLES-1213 (b. 1550-Iden, S, E, United Kingdom d. Deceased)

Anne WENHAM-1021 (b. 2 Oct 1608-Chalvington, Sussex, England d. 1681-Sussex, E, United Kingdom)
┌ Mr. SAINTGEORGE-1214 (b. 1548-C, Sussex, England d. Deceased-England)
Anne SAINTGEORGE-1211 (b. 1570-Chalvington, S, England d. Deceased)
└ Mrs. SAINTGEORGE-1215 (b. 1548-C, Sussex, England d. Deceased-England)

James BOOTES-290 (b. 21 May 1699-Burwash, Sussex, England d. 13 Aug 1741-Bodiam, Sussex, England)
└ Susanna -566 (b. Abt 1647-Sussex, England d. Deceased)

Bartholomew BOOTS-134 (b. 25 Apr 1736-Bodiam, Sussex, England d. 16 Sep 1806-Northiam, Sussex, England)
┌ COLLINS-1219 (b. Abt 1610-England, United Kingdom d. Deceased)
Thomas COLLINS-1022 (b. Abt 1644-Burwash, Sussex, England d. Deceased)
└ Mrs. Collins -1220 (b. Abt 1615-England, United Kingdom d. Deceased)

William COLLINS-567 (b. 5 Jun 1672-Bodiam, Sussex, England d. Deceased)
└ Margaret -1023 (b. Abt 1649-Burwash, Sussex, E, United Kingdom d. Deceased)

Anne COLLINS-291 (b. 4 Nov 1693-Bodiam, Sussex, England d. Aft 1736-Bodiam, Sussex, England)
┌ SMERSALL-1246 (b. Abt 1510-E, United Kingdom d. Deceased)
John SMERSALL-1228 (b. Abt 1538-B, S, , United Kingdom d. Deceased)
└ Mrs. Smersall -1247 (b. Abt 1515-England, United Kingdom d. Deceased)

John SMERSALL-1223 (b. Abt 1568-B, S, , United Kingdom d. Deceased)
└ Bedreas PRETTLE-1229 (d. 19 Nov 1592)

John SMERSALL the Third-1221 (b. Abt 1604-B, S, , United Kingdom d. Deceased)
┌ Georgii CHESMAN-1232 (b. Abt 1540-Brede, Sussex, E, United Kingdom d. Deceased)
Margaret CHESMAN-1224 (b. 1575-B, S, , United Kingdom d. Deceased)
┌ William COOPER-1248 (b. Abt 1523-Brede, Sussex, England d. Deceased)
Bridget COOPER-1233 (b. Abt 1543-B, S, , United Kingdom d. Aft 1593)
└ Mrs William COOPER-1249 (b. Abt 1527-Brede, Sussex, England d. Deceased)

William SMERSWELL-1024 (b. Abt 1630-B, S, E, United Kingdom d. Deceased)
┌ Walter BOURNE OR BORNE-1264 (b. Abt 1474-W, W, England d. Aft 1532-)
┌ John BOURNE-1250 (b. 1500-B, Essex, England d. 1561-Bobbingworth, E, England)
William BOURNE-1234 (b. Abt 1527-Bobbingworth, Essex, England d. 29 Apr 1591-)
└ Margaret -1251 (b. 1505-Bobbingworth, E, England d. 1564-England)

Ancestors of Joseph Franklin GOODSELL-8

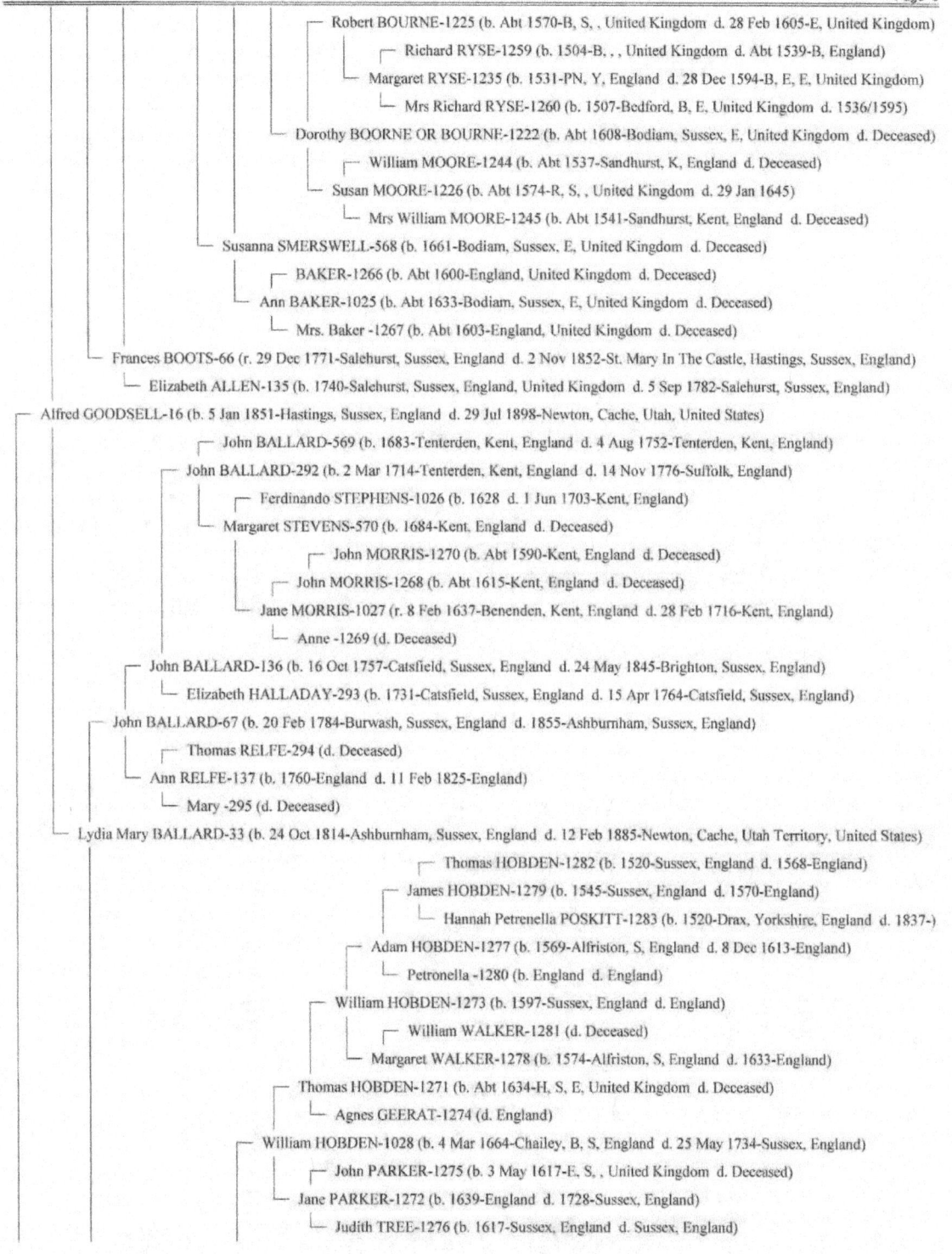

Robert BOURNE-1225 (b. Abt 1570-B, S, , United Kingdom d. 28 Feb 1605-E, United Kingdom)

Richard RYSE-1259 (b. 1504-B, , , United Kingdom d. Abt 1539-B, England)

Margaret RYSE-1235 (b. 1531-PN, Y, England d. 28 Dec 1594-B, E, E, United Kingdom)

Mrs Richard RYSE-1260 (b. 1507-Bedford, B, E, United Kingdom d. 1536/1595)

Dorothy BOORNE OR BOURNE-1222 (b. Abt 1608-Bodiam, Sussex, E, United Kingdom d. Deceased)

William MOORE-1244 (b. Abt 1537-Sandhurst, K, England d. Deceased)

Susan MOORE-1226 (b. Abt 1574-R, S, , United Kingdom d. 29 Jan 1645)

Mrs William MOORE-1245 (b. Abt 1541-Sandhurst, Kent, England d. Deceased)

Susanna SMERSWELL-568 (b. 1661-Bodiam, Sussex, E, United Kingdom d. Deceased)

BAKER-1266 (b. Abt 1600-England, United Kingdom d. Deceased)

Ann BAKER-1025 (b. Abt 1633-Bodiam, Sussex, E, United Kingdom d. Deceased)

Mrs. Baker -1267 (b. Abt 1603-England, United Kingdom d. Deceased)

Frances BOOTS-66 (r. 29 Dec 1771-Salehurst, Sussex, England d. 2 Nov 1852-St. Mary In The Castle, Hastings, Sussex, England)

Elizabeth ALLEN-135 (b. 1740-Salehurst, Sussex, England, United Kingdom d. 5 Sep 1782-Salehurst, Sussex, England)

Alfred GOODSELL-16 (b. 5 Jan 1851-Hastings, Sussex, England d. 29 Jul 1898-Newton, Cache, Utah, United States)

John BALLARD-569 (b. 1683-Tenterden, Kent, England d. 4 Aug 1752-Tenterden, Kent, England)

John BALLARD-292 (b. 2 Mar 1714-Tenterden, Kent, England d. 14 Nov 1776-Suffolk, England)

Ferdinando STEPHENS-1026 (b. 1628 d. 1 Jun 1703-Kent, England)

Margaret STEVENS-570 (b. 1684-Kent, England d. Deceased)

John MORRIS-1270 (b. Abt 1590-Kent, England d. Deceased)

John MORRIS-1268 (b. Abt 1615-Kent, England d. Deceased)

Jane MORRIS-1027 (r. 8 Feb 1637-Benenden, Kent, England d. 28 Feb 1716-Kent, England)

Anne -1269 (d. Deceased)

John BALLARD-136 (b. 16 Oct 1757-Catsfield, Sussex, England d. 24 May 1845-Brighton, Sussex, England)

Elizabeth HALLADAY-293 (b. 1731-Catsfield, Sussex, England d. 15 Apr 1764-Catsfield, Sussex, England)

John BALLARD-67 (b. 20 Feb 1784-Burwash, Sussex, England d. 1855-Ashburnham, Sussex, England)

Thomas RELFE-294 (d. Deceased)

Ann RELFE-137 (b. 1760-England d. 11 Feb 1825-England)

Mary -295 (d. Deceased)

Lydia Mary BALLARD-33 (b. 24 Oct 1814-Ashburnham, Sussex, England d. 12 Feb 1885-Newton, Cache, Utah Territory, United States)

Thomas HOBDEN-1282 (b. 1520-Sussex, England d. 1568-England)

James HOBDEN-1279 (b. 1545-Sussex, England d. 1570-England)

Hannah Petrenella POSKITT-1283 (b. 1520-Drax, Yorkshire, England d. 1837-)

Adam HOBDEN-1277 (b. 1569-Alfriston, S, England d. 8 Dec 1613-England)

Petronella -1280 (b. England d. England)

William HOBDEN-1273 (b. 1597-Sussex, England d. England)

William WALKER-1281 (d. Deceased)

Margaret WALKER-1278 (b. 1574-Alfriston, S, England d. 1633-England)

Thomas HOBDEN-1271 (b. Abt 1634-H, S, E, United Kingdom d. Deceased)

Agnes GEERAT-1274 (d. England)

William HOBDEN-1028 (b. 4 Mar 1664-Chailey, B, S, England d. 25 May 1734-Sussex, England)

John PARKER-1275 (b. 3 May 1617-E, S, , United Kingdom d. Deceased)

Jane PARKER-1272 (b. 1639-England d. 1728-Sussex, England)

Judith TREE-1276 (b. 1617-Sussex, England d. Sussex, England)

Ancestors of Joseph Franklin GOODSELL-8

Thomas HOBDEN-571 (b. 1700-Sussex, England, United Kingdom d. 16 Jan 1768-Maresfield, Sussex, England)

John BRIGHTRIDGE-1293 (b. Abt 1648-Barcombe, S, England d. Deceased)

Mary BRIGHTRIDGE-1029 (b. Abt 1668-Barcombe, Sussex, England d. 3 Jun 1712-Sussex, England)

Ellinor CARMAN-1294 (b. Abt 1652-Barcombe, Sussex, England d. Deceased)

Edward HOBDEN-300 (b. 27 Aug 1732-Maresfield, Sussex, England d. 24 Dec 1808-Maresfield, Sussex, England)

Catherine HUMPHREY-572 (b. 1700-Sussex, England, United Kingdom d. Deceased)

Richard HOBDEN-138 (b. Abt 1756-Penhurst, Sussex, England, United Kingdom d. Deceased)

Thomas BERWICK-573 (b. 1700-Sussex, England d. Jul 1770-Buxted, Sussex, England)

Ann BERWICK-301 (b. Abt 1728-Maresfield, Sussex, England d. 1806)

John GLAZIER-1030 (b. 1682-England d. England)

Lucy GLAZIER-574 (b. 1704-Buxted, Sussex, England d. Sep 1767-Buxted, Sussex, England)

Ambrose DURRANT-1295 (d. Deceased)

Elizabeth DURRANT-1031 (b. 1684-England d. England)

Mary HOBDEN-68 (b. 2 Feb 1790-Battle, Sussex, England d. 15 Mar 1833-Ashburnham, Sussex, England)

Elizabeth VINCENT-139 (b. Abt 1760-Penhurst, Sussex, England d. 5 May 1830-Penhurst, Sussex, England)

Joseph Franklin GOODSELL-8 (b. 21 Feb 1886-Newton, Cache, UT, United States d. 21 Sep 1934-PA, C, W, United States)

Jens -575 (b. 1710-Vejby, Frederiksborg, Denmark d. Deceased)

Christopher JENSEN-302 (b. 1735-Tibirke, Tibirke, Frederiksborg, Denmark d. Deceased)

Mads CHRISTOPHERSEN-140 (b. Abt 1761-Vejby, Frederiksborg, Denmark d. 14 Jun 1845-Vejby, Frederiksborg, Denmark)

Hans -576 (b. 1710-Tibirke, Tibirke, Frederiksborg, Denmark d. Deceased)

Kirsten HANSDATTER-303 (b. 1735-Tibirke, Tibirke, Frederiksborg, Denmark d. Deceased)

Jens MADSEN-69 (b. Abt 1799-Vejby, Frederiksborg, Denmark d. 27 Apr 1841-Vejby, Frederiksborg, Denmark)

Lars -577 (b. 1695-Vejby, Vejby, Frederiksborg, Denmark d. Deceased)

Niels LARSEN-305 (b. 1717-Denmark d. Deceased)

Bertha NIELSDATTER-141 (b. Abt 1771-Vejby, Frederiksborg, Denmark d. 1814)

Christians -578 (b. 1705-Vejby, Vejby, Frederiksborg, Denmark d. Deceased)

Birthe CHRISTIANSDATTER-306 (b. Abt 1731-Vejby, Frederiksborg, Denmark d. Denmark)

Nelie -579 (b. 1705-Vejby, Frederiksborg, Denmark d. Deceased)

Hans JENSEN-34 (b. 6 Aug 1825-Vejby, Holbo, Frederiksborg, Denmark d. Vejby, Vejby, Holbo, Frederiksborg, Denmark)

Niels -580 (b. 1680-Tågerup, Ramløse, Frederiksborg, Denmark d. Deceased)

Christen NIELSEN-308 (b. Abt 1705-Tågerup, Ramløse, Frederiksborg, Denmark d. Deceased)

Karen -581 (b. 1680-Tågerup, Ramløse, Frederiksborg, Denmark d. Deceased)

Hans CHRISTENSEN-142 (b. Abt 1754-Tågerup, Ramløse, Frederiksborg, Denmark d. 20 Aug 1814-Tågerup, R, F, Denmark)

Hans -582 (b. 1685-Tågerup, Ramløse, Frederiksborg, Denmark d. Deceased)

Kirsten HANSEN-309 (b. Abt 1709-Tågerup, Ramløse, Frederiksborg, Denmark d. Deceased)

Maren -583 (b. 1685-Tågerup, Ramløse, Frederiksborg, Denmark d. Deceased)

Pernille HANSDATTER-70 (b. 4 Mar 1789-Tågerup, Ramløse, Frederiksborg, Denmark d. 13 Jun 1867-Vejby, F, Denmark)

Jorgens -584 (b. 1710-Ramløse, Frederiksborg, Denmark d. Deceased)

Lars JORGENSEN-310 (b. Abt 1733-Ramløse, Frederiksborg, Denmark d. Deceased)

Johanne -585 (b. 1710-Ramløse, Frederiksborg, Denmark d. Deceased)

Susanne LARSDATTER-143 (b. Abt 1748-Ramløse, Frederiksborg, Denmark d. 20 Feb 1819)

Mads -586 (b. 1710-Ramløse, Frederiksborg, Denmark d. Deceased)

Pernille MADSDATTER-311 (b. Abt 1737-Ramløse, Frederiksborg, Denmark d. Deceased)

Susanne -587 (b. 1710-Ramløse, Frederiksborg, Denmark d. Deceased)

└─ Hannah Christina JENSEN-17 (b. 24 Aug 1853-Mønge, Vejby, Frederiksborg, Denmark d. 17 Jun 1888-Newton, Cache, UT, United States)

```
                        ┌─ Lars HANSEN-312 (b. Abt 1731-Husby, Vends, Odense, Denmark  d. Deceased)
                ┌─ Niels LARSEN-144 (b. 5 Jun 1757-Håre, Tanderup, Båg, Odense, Denmark  d. 14 Mar 1846-Husby, H, V, Odense, Denmark)
        ┌─ Lars NIELSEN-71 (b. 14 Jan 1793-Husby, Husby, Odense, Denmark  d. 17 May 1872-Kindstrup, Gelsted, Vends, Odense, Denmark)
        │       └─ Maren HANSDATTER-145 (b. 1769  d. Bef 1834)
   ┌─ Maren LARSDATTER-35 (b. 29 Jul 1830-Mønge, Vejby, Holbo, Frederiksborg, Denmark  d. 9 Feb 1906-Newton, Cache, U, United States)
   │                            ┌─ Peder -1296 (b. Abt 1630  d. Deceased)
   │                    ┌─ Terchel PEDERSEN-1032 (b. Abt 1644-of Roile, Vejlby, Denmark  d. 1713-R, VS, V, Odense Amt, Denmark)
   │            ┌─ Peder TERCHELSEN-588 (b. 1675-Røjle, VS, VH, Odense Amt, Denmark  d. 1740-R, V, , Odense Amt, Denmark)
   │        ┌─ Soren PEDERSEN-313 (b. 10 May 1722-Vejlby, Odense, Denmark  d. 25 May 1798-Gelsted, Odense, Denmark)
   │        │       └─ Bodil RASMUSDATTER-589 (b. 1680  d. Deceased)
   │    ┌─ Hans SORENSEN-146 (r. 17 Jun 1759-Vejlby, Odense, Denmark  d. 26 Mar 1849-Kindstrup, Gelsted, Odense, Denmark)
   │    │        ┌─ Hans ANDERSEN-590 (b. Abt 1695  d. Deceased)
   │    │    └─ Mette Sophie HANSEN-314 (b. Abt 1720-Vejlby, Odense, Denmark  d. 13 Sep 1793-Kindstrup, Gelsted, O, Denmark)
   │    │                    ┌─ Anders POUFVELSEN-1297 (d. Deceased)
   │    │            ┌─ Poufvel ANDERSEN-1033 (r. 17 Jan 1664-Indslev, Odense, Denmark  d. Deceased)
   │    │        └─ Maren POVELSEN-591 (b. Abt 1694-Middelfart, Odense, Denmark  d. 19 Jun 1753-Vejlby, Odense, Denmark)
   │    │                └─ Anne HANSEN-1034 (d. Deceased)
   └─ Anne Catrine HANSEN-72 (b. 27 Jun 1801-Kindstrup, Gelsted, Odense, Denmark  d. 14 Jan 1841-Gelsted, Odense, Denmark)
        │        ┌─ Lauritz MADSEN-592 (b. 1705-Strandby, Ålborg, Denmark  d. Deceased)
        │    ┌─ Mads LAURITZSEN-315 (b. Abt 1736-Gelsted, Odense, Denmark  d. 19 Aug 1818-Gelsted, Odense, Denmark)
        │    │        ┌─ Jens CHRISTENSEN-1035 (b. <1695>-Aalborg, Denmark  d. Deceased)
        │    │    └─ Mette JENSEN-593 (b. 7 Apr 1713-Ullits, Ålborg, Denmark  d. 11 Mar 1761-Ullits, Ålborg, Denmark)
        │    │        └─ Annie NIELSDATTER-1036 (b. <1699>-Aalborg, Denmark  d. Deceased)
        └─ Kirsten MADSEN-147 (b. 20 Nov 1768-Gelsted, Odense, Denmark  d. 19 Oct 1837-Gelsted, Odense, Denmark)
             │                    ┌─ _____ Laurs... -1298 (b. Abt 1636-Skaade, Aarhus, Denmark  d. Deceased)
             │            ┌─ Peder LAURSEN-1039 (b. Abt 1661-Sønderup, Sorø, Denmark  d. Apr 1736-Skaade, Aarhus, Denmark)
             │            │    └─ Mrs. Laurs -1299 (b. Abt 1640-Of Skaade, Holme, Denmark  d. Deceased)
             │        ┌─ Mads PEDERSEN-594 (b. 1693-Skaade, Aarhus, Denmark  d. 23 Nov 1755-Skaade, Aarhus, Denmark)
             │        │    └─ Mrs. Peder LAURSEN-1040 (b. Abt 1665-Fana, Hordaland, Norway  d. Deceased)
             └─ Anne Catrine MADSDATTER-316 (b. 1737-Skaade, Aarhus, Denmark  d. 7 Jun 1790-Gelsted, Odense, Denmark)
                  │        ┌─ Rasmus -1041 (b. Abt 1674-Fulden, Beder, Århus, Denmark  d. Deceased)
                  └─ Anne Cathrine RASMUSDATTER-595 (b. 1700-Beder, Aarhus, Denmark  d. 28 Nov 1762)
                       └─ Mrs- Rasmus -1042 (b. Abt 1676-Fulden, Beder, Århus, Denmark  d. Deceased)
```

Dedication

This book is dedicated to my children, Malissa, Clayton, and Emma.